AUG 11 1995

toward a new psychology of women

Jean Baker Miller, M.D.

toward a new psychology of women
Second Edition

BEACON PRESS / BOSTON

Beacon Press
25 Beacon Street
Boston, Massachusetts 02108

Beacon Press books are published under the auspices
of the Unitarian Universalist Association
of Congregations in North America.

92 91 90 89 88   8 7 6 5 4 3 2

Portions of Chapters 1 and 2 were previously published
in another form in the paper "Psychological Consequences
of Sexual Inequality," in the *American Journal of Orthopsychiatry,* 41 (1971), 767–775, copyright held by the
American Orthopsychiatric Association, Inc.

Library of Congress Cataloging-in-Publication Data

Miller, Jean Baker.
    Toward a new psychology of women.

    Bibliography: p.
    Includes index.
    1. Women—Psychology. I. Title.
HQ1206.M52 1986   155.6'33   86–47553
ISBN 0–8070–2910–6
ISBN 0–8070–2909–2 (pbk.)

This book is for Helen Merrell Lynd

contents

foreword to
the second edition

The most important thing to do in this new foreword is to thank the women and men who wrote or spoke to me about this book. Their words would make a more valuable contribution than anything I can write here. They portray the very texture and fabric of many lives, in all of their richness and variation.

One of the letters came from a woman who read the book while she was in prison. She said she now could make sense of her life — of what had happened to her and why. She developed an analysis of the forces affecting her and the reasons for her actions. Another letter was from a black professional woman who said that she had been very successful by the usual standards. She wrote that she was dying of cancer. She was glad, she said, that her life had encompassed the civil rights movement of the 1960s and 1970s and the black writers emerging from it because she now understood her life in the context of the black experience in the United States. She, like many successful women, black and white, had not thought there was anything more she needed to understand about women as women. However, she still had felt much anger and anguish and believed these reflected her personal deficiencies. After reading the book, she put together her experiences as a woman and as a black person. "I now can die without bitterness," she wrote.

I am extraordinarily grateful to these readers for many reasons, but one special reason above all: they went beyond the book. They carried forward many complex formulations. Often they disagreed with me. They used the book as

Foreword

a take-off point. That was my main hope. Because many people did these things, they have helped me.

Ten years ago, two intertwined motives impelled me to write this book. For one, in clinical practice for many years, I had heard women talk of their concern with what seemed to me the most important things in life — for example, the real emotions flowing between people or women's worries about how their activities were affecting those close to them. From these kinds of concerns and from their daily lives, women developed psychological qualities that were extraordinarily valuable but that went unrecognized. If psychiatrists and psychologists noticed these characteristics at all, they described them in distorted terms that did not capture their essence. They tended to cast women's activity in disparaging molds, such as "being too dependent on the reactions of others," rather than in more accurate language such as "being able to encompass the experiences and well-being of the other." Women's valuable characteristics are common, not rare. They exist in abundance in "ordinary women." Often women themselves don't notice them, and they are diverted away from noticing them — systematically.

Thus, there was, and still is, a dilemma. This abundance of women's psychological strengths exists but cannot flourish or come forward fully into a world that sorely needs *precisely* these kinds of strengths. And women themselves cannot really believe in them, give them credence, and draw on them as a basis for their development and growth. Why do women not recognize these important parts of themselves? The task, then, was to begin a description of women's strengths and to account for the reasons that they went unrecognized. I believe that this is still a major task before us. Out of this can follow a new framework for understanding women — and men.

The second and related reason for embarking on this book ten years ago was that the model of the new woman seemed to many people to be the model of the man. While this was not what all women leaders and writers were saying,

Foreword

it was what many people seemed to be hearing. Some women writers were, and still are, implicitly accepting the model of the man as the only model of a seemingly full-fledged person. The mass and professional media certainly played a role in conveying this impression to a great many women and to men as well. The goal that women should become men or even become *like* men seemed disastrous to me for many reasons. Therefore, it seemed important to begin to create new images and visions and to explain the reasons why we needed new visions rather than imitations of old models. And the place to start was to describe the actual life activities and values of the vast majority of women.

Setting out on that path led to a central point in this book — the notion that our understanding of all of life has been underdeveloped and distorted because our past explanations have been created by only one half of the human species. We can already glimpse fuller and richer explanations.

How does this picture look ten years later? Are these issues still important? I believe they are. However, a large amount of new knowledge has come to us in the last decade and we have seen many changes in reality in these ten years. It is important to reflect on these changes because we are able to glimpse new insight only as we change the way we act.

In the last decade it has become clearer that if women are trying to define and create a full personhood, we are engaged in a huge undertaking. We see that this attempt means building a new way of living which encompasses all realms of life, from global economic, social, and political levels to the most intimate personal relationships. We do not accomplish such a thoroughgoing task easily or quickly. If we take women's situation seriously, we cannot think in terms of a fast solution. Perhaps we need a twofold perspective, thinking in terms of both urgent actions and a very long process. Perhaps this perspective will help us to not be discouraged about the pace. Given the profound ways in which

Foreword

the female-male situation is inscribed into all of life, all the necessary change is not likely to occur readily and rapidly.

Viewing women's situation in this light, we can see that women have made remarkable progress in many areas. In proportion to all that needs changing, however, the advances are not nearly enough. Thus, the picture is very mixed.[1]

Women of all ages and at different phases of life face a variety of issues today. One of the terrible features of the past was that women were told to be "all one way," as in "the only right thing for a real woman to be is a wife and mother." A danger today is that some people advocate another form of "the right thing," as in "the only right thing to do is to strive unstintingly for a high-powered career." The high-powered career as currently defined — for men — did not arise from the life experience and desires that most women experience; and many women and men have posed serious questions about how beneficial this mode of life is for men. Women have begun to celebrate the variety of ways of being in the world that different women have constructed and have been encouraging each other to continue to create and enjoy them. In many instances, however, very real pressures push women into old molds. It would help to keep delineating these pressures and to work to alter them if we see them as noxious.

Women are now participating in different realms of life in numbers that seemed almost impossible to imagine ten to fifteen years ago — they attend medical school, law school, and business school and hold positions in professions and corporations previously closed to them. Current evidence suggests, however, that women may reach the lower echelons of professions or corporations but that most of these institutions prevent them from moving higher. Women have described the complicated problems and obstacles they face in the stages that follow the first step of merely "getting in" to these positions. In addition, many women seriously question the values and procedures of our current institu-

Foreword

tions. The ways they are required to operate and to treat colleagues and their own families conflict with deeply held values. Women are entering a work scene that is not likely to be totally fulfilling. It is important to analyze it as accurately as possible.[2] The great danger at this time is that women assume they are deficient because they don't "fit in" with ease. If women feel conflict about job situations, there is usually good reason for it.[3]

More important, the advances in the work world demonstrate gains for the more advantaged groups of women and maybe a few from the lower classes. The vast majority of working women, 80 percent, hold the lowest-paid and most dead-end jobs in this country. Women in many other countries work in much worse conditions than those found in the United States. In addition, in the United States and elsewhere, cutbacks in many public programs have deprived low-income women even further by limiting health care, child care, school lunch programs, and a variety of other services. These services were not sufficient even before the recent reductions.[4] We do not yet speak in a strong enough voice for this *majority* of women. We must continue to point to this basic economic situation as the greatest need.

In this decade, too, women of color in the United States and throughout the world have brought forward their perspectives more fully and forcefully. They have shown also that women of the whole world are connected in an economic and political dynamic that continues to force the poorest women of the world into worsening economic conditions. Women of the developing world have given us a global vision. They have shown us that the concerns of all women are linked in the most fundamental way.[5]

We cannot expect strong gains for women if the majority of women are not participating in or enjoying the advances. I do not think that the added advantages which have come to the already advantaged women in the last decade will be sustained unless the large majority of women begin to share in them.

Foreword

At the same time, however, we can pay great honor to the women who have worked enormously hard on issues which affect working-class and poor women nationally and internationally. Many working-class, poor, and professional women have worked together to improve women's wages, working conditions, benefits, pensions, unemployment, housing, child care, legal rights, and other basic needs. Women have helped each other to gain and improve jobs in both the traditional women's fields and the nontraditional fields. In the United States, several organizations such as Nine to Five, the Coalition of Labor Union Women, and the National Commission on Working Women have pointed the way. Women in these and other organizations have made gains against strong resistance, and many women have become inspired to struggle in new ways. But the changes have not yet been enough to improve conditions for the majority of women in the face of the powerful forces at work in the general economy.

Women have made great change in other areas which reach across class and racial lines. One area is violence against women. Before women began their major effort on issues such as rape, battering of women, child sexual abuse, and incest, almost no one paid attention to these violent crimes. Many people didn't believe they occurred. As a result, women were silenced or worse — if they tried to speak out about these issues, they were usually doubly punished by the mistreatment they received from law enforcement agencies, courts, clinics, hospitals, superiors at the workplace, and others. Often, this is still the case. However, actions initiated by women, such as rape crisis centers and programs for battered women, have given women a place to turn and have created a voice on the public scene. These programs have reached poor women. While all women are at risk, poor women suffer most from lack of public protection and attention to widespread violence.

In the face of massive societal acceptance of and simultaneous silence about violence toward women, it has taken

Foreword

enormous effort to bring the truth to light, to demonstrate that these violations are not rare but common. Doing something about them has taken even more effort. It is still very hard to keep women's programs going, even harder with the present widespread cutbacks. Instead of reductions, we need more funding for more encompassing programs. And we need basic change not only to help victims but to end the victimization — to make it impossible that such violations occur in the first place.

One of the most important advances which has occurred is that many women have come together with a new sense of themselves as women. This is a vast change from the time when women were unable to see much value or importance in themselves or each other, when women were focused on men as the important people. Women's outlook is very different today from what it was only ten to fifteen years ago. The psychological ramifications are momentous because it is true, as many women have said, that in devaluing other women, women inevitably devalue themselves. Women still have not fully overcome this devaluation. There are still few women who can believe deeply that they are truly worthy. Likewise, the process of valuing other women has not reached full fruition, and new kinds of problems arise as women begin to come together in new ways. Women have differences on some major issues. Perhaps we have begun to understand that women cannot overcome centuries of separation from each other without the surfacing of significant problems and without developing new ways of attending to them. Most important are the differences caused by race, class, and sexual preference. Despite these new problems, a basic psychological process has been set in motion.

At the same time that we recognize that women have just begun to act for and from themselves, we see that a backlash has arisen in reaction to even partial change. A backlash may be an indication that women really have had an effect, but backlashes occur when advances have been small, before changes are sufficient to help many people. For example, women have been blamed for the "breakdown of the family" or for all the problems of youth, drugs, crime, and unemployment. Women have not hurt or deprived the people who lead the backlash. It is almost as if the leaders of backlashes use the fear of change as a threat before major change has occurred. Some have suggested that the backlash against women has been made even more cogent because women are such an emotionally charged topic, such a ready target for politicians and others to use for their own self-seeking goals. The problems blamed on women stem from deep-seated sources which are not determined by women at all; instead, women are the victims of them.[6]

Thus, we are in a period of great flux, a time of transition with trends in several directions. Many people have worked hard to solve problems only to find new sets of problems emerging. Many women and men have struggled to effect profound personal change. Some are trying to succeed in workplaces which do not begin to encompass women's experience and values. Many women, along with male allies, have tried to change political, economic, social, cultural, and religious institutions, but these powerful structures do not change readily; they respond with powerful counterreactions. Each new step reveals the necessity of analyzing more deeply the cultural and psychological forces impinging on us all. Each new step makes us aware of the energy and courage still demanded.

In the context of this mixed picture, what has happened in the last decade to aid our psychological understanding? One striking feature is the vast outpouring of literature in psychology as well as other fields — the new scholarship on women. The volume and quality of this literature testify to the storehouse of creativity which was there to be revealed and the riches which continue to flow. This literature stands as a glowing tribute to the gifts and energies of many, many women. It also demonstrates that people's creativity flourishes when the surrounding milieu begins to nourish it. The societal conditions are still far from fully encouraging, however. Most of the members of the professional and academic world still do not consider the study of women to be serious work. They view it as secondary or peripheral at best. They do not perceive the obvious implications for the total human community, for all society, for men as well as women. Or perhaps they glimpse this profundity and perceive it as threatening. Perhaps this fear accounts in part for their disparagement of this work, even when some of it is brilliant and almost all of it stimulating. Thus, while there are some notable exceptions, most of the academic and professional worlds do not support and encourage the exciting new scholarship on women. These worlds do not invite women to help them learn, to help them enlarge and improve their theories and practice. Similarly, teaching in most fields does not incorporate the vast amount of new scholarship into the central body of knowledge. Certainly training programs for mental health professionals do not do so. They relegate scholarship on women to the periphery, to be found only by those who make a special effort to seek it out and who do so under the general notion that they must be doing something unimportant — and they must therefore be "unimportant people." Despite this attempt to ignore or downplay the work being done, many women professionals and significant numbers of men have learned from this new knowledge and are profoundly affected by it; this is a new phenomenon.

Outside of academia and the professions, large numbers of women and men seek out the new knowledge that women are creating and keep it alive and growing. They now know things they never knew before and have enriched their lives and understanding immeasurably. Moreover, women meet in large organizations and small groups in many occupational and professional fields. Journals, newspapers, and newsletters continue to emerge as important forms of communication. New perspectives have developed in women's groups in other settings as well — such as churches, synagogues, unions, and neighborhood and political organiza-

Foreword

tions. From all of these settings comes the encouragement that is essential for the continued development of more knowledge.

In the large body of new literature on the psychology of women, many writers have brought us a wealth of new knowledge. I will highlight only two major themes. One is the growing tendency to focus on the close study of women and to describe women's lives and women's development in the terms in which it is lived rather than to force it into the categories which we have inherited, categories that originated in the attempt by men to describe all of life. In the largest sense, all of our prior thinking emerged from men's institutions and men's ways of perceiving. In the last decade, women have begun to study women and men in ways that shift this base.

The other major trend is the increasing elucidation of the psychological effects of sexual violence on all women — and men as well. By noting this work, I do not imply an evaluation of all the important work women have done in psychology. These are the two areas which connect to my own concerns at present.

Over time, we can see certain characteristics in the writings of members of an oppressed group. Initially, many writers work to dispel the false ideas which have been purveyed about the group. Dispelling falsities is very valuable. Along with it, however, a tendency often emerges to "prove" that the oppressed group is "just as good as the so-called first rate people" and should be treated in the same way. In seeking to prove this, writers often accept the standards and values of the dominant group, either wittingly or unwittingly. They often assume that the dominant group's method of advancing knowledge is the best or only method. Indeed, academic disciplines exert heavy pressure on everyone to believe this, and they tend to penalize and silence those who deviate from it.

Once the period of dispelling falsities is under way, the ability emerges to see the experience of the oppressed or "second-class people" in their own terms — and to see that these terms can open up a greater understanding not only of the second-class people but of everyone. It then becomes clearer that the categories and even the words used by the dominant group are not appropriate. The words usually tend to systematically downgrade and obscure the experience of the subordinate group and to misrepresent the experience of the dominant group. If writers search for more appropriate terms, they depart from the usual categories and assumptions. They then see the experience of the dominant group in a new light, in terms that can illuminate that experience as well as the total human experience.

This new scholarship leads to the recognition that the descriptions of the events occurring in the lives of the subordinate group were inadequate, as were those used to describe the dominant group. A new set of assumptions emerges. The point is not that women immediately know or understand everything. The dominant-subordinate situation was — and is — depriving and distorting to members of both sexes, but in different ways for each. The point is that the close study of an oppressed group reveals that a dominant group inevitably describes a subordinate group falsely in terms derived from its own systems of thought. These same false categories guide the dominant group's explanations about itself. Once writers see the inadequacy of these terms, they have to find new ones. And once they begin to find new ones, they see that the systems of thought which contained such false terms are seriously flawed in their basic assumptions, which had previously defined everything.

Perhaps I can illustrate this point by a brief reference to my own concerns in the past ten years. I have become even more convinced that the study of women's specific psychological development opens up paths to a better understanding of all psychological development, particularly those aspects which are most obscure. If we look at what women have been doing in life, we see that a large part of it can be called "active participation in the development of others." This participation occurs in the daily interactions in which most women engage all of the time with adults as well as children. One way of describing what women do is to say that women try to interact with others in ways which will foster the other person's development in many psychological dimensions, that is, emotionally, intellectually, and so on. This kind of interaction builds the other person's psychological resources. Professionals use words such as "mothering," "nurturing," "care-taking," and the like to characterize this activity. (Sometimes they have not seen it as activity at all but have made it appear to be a form of "passivity"!) These terms do not begin to describe the very complex activity involved.

Another way to describe this activity is to say that women try to use their powers, that is, their intellectual and emotional abilities, to empower others, to build other people's strength, resources, effectiveness, and well-being.[7] All women do not succeed all of the time, but they try.

No one grows at all without these kinds of interactions. However, psychologists have not concentrated on gaining accurate knowledge of women's experience in these interactions even though psychological development is a central concern in the field. Also, women themselves have not been encouraged to grant them full and true value.

Psychologists use terms such as "merger," "fusion," "attachment," or "dependency" to characterize the child's early relationship with its mother and terms such as "separation," "independence," and "autonomy" in speaking of maturity or the end point of development. None of these terms focuses on the nature of the interaction at each age. Indeed, the words do not bespeak interaction. A term such as "fusion" conveys no interaction; nor does a term such as "independence." Likewise, the criteria for maturity do not include the ability to engage in interactions which empower others and, simultaneously, oneself. The implication is that

the "mature, independent person" will also make "good relationships" because "he" will have built a strong inner psychological structure, but we know that there are few such
strong, independent persons and if we do see one, many
other persons are usually helping him to survive and
function.[8]

While it is obvious that all of living and all of development
takes place only within relationships, our theories of development seem to rest at bottom on a notion of development
as a process of separating from others. I believe this notion
stems from an illusion, a fiction which men, but not women,
are encouraged to pursue. In general, women have been
assigned to the realms of life concerned with building relationships, especially relationships that foster development.
Thus, from the study of women's lives we can begin to gain
a greater understanding of growth-enhancing interactions.
We can see, too, the obstacles that prevent the full realiza-
tion of these interactions. We perceive the deficiencies and
problems in men's development in a new way.[9]

Women have not created a comprehensive new psychological theory, and we do not yet have a set of more appropriate categories and words. There is no easy leaping over
the only systems of thought and language that we have inherited. But we are now becoming increasingly aware of the
need for new assumptions and new words. We perceive that
the close study of women's experience can lead eventually
to a new synthesis which will better describe all experience.
The women writers who are ready to depart from the most
sacred assumptions are extending our vision of the human
possibilities.[10]

The exposure of violence in women's lives and its psychological effect on everyone, not only the direct victims, has
also intensified over the past ten years. This body of literature deserves special honor because the women who spear-
headed it were themselves survivors of violence or women
whose writing grew out of direct action to change the situ-

Foreword

ation, or both.[11] Their work has produced remarkable results and has opened up a whole field of study that continues to require great efforts.

According to the data so far available, we now have estimates that rape occurs to one out of four women in the United States, that one third of female children and adolescents under the age of eighteen experience significant sexual abuse,[12] and that violence occurs in one third to one half of U.S. families.[13] Major efforts were required to find out this information because the overwhelming number of beatings and instances of sexual abuse and harassment are never reported and counted.[14]

Not only have writers revealed the violence against women, some have voiced the more extensive proposition that all women grow up within a context that includes the threat of violence, particularly sexualized violence. This threat not only affects the women who are directly hurt but reaches every child growing up in every family. Thus, incest and sexual abuse of children is far more common than we ever suspected. And, as Judith Herman suggests, evidence of such widespread violations of young girls and the frequent powerlessness of their mothers elucidates a threat that exists in all families.[15]

This work on violence adds a major dimension to my discussion of inequality in this book. One of my points in this book is that we can understand much of what happens to women if we see how women have been socially defined as unequals, similar to other people who have been designated second class on the bases of class, race, and religion. Such a framework helps to explain a great deal about women and also helps to alter the tendency to assign psychological causes in inappropriate ways.

Additional forces are at work, however, in the man-woman situation because of its personal nature and intensity. Our culture teaches most people to seek the fulfillment of their deepest needs and desires within this relationship.

Foreword

Further, this relationship has been the basis of the family, in which the mind of each generation is formed. In the first edition of this book, I did not give sufficient weight to the factor of violence in this situation.

Even as women live with the pervasive threat of violence, they develop extremely valuable psychological characteristics because they continue to try to create growth-fostering interactions within the family and in other settings. Women, as a group, struggle to create life-giving and life-enhancing relationships within a context of violence and life-destroying forces.

My own work at this time centers on trying to understand more about the nature of "relational contexts" and "relational modes" which foster psychological development. I feel very fortunate to be able to do this work with several colleagues who share a general approach and whose work appears in the Working Paper Series produced by the Stone Center for Developmental Studies and Services at Wellesley College. At times, our ideas flow from the interactions among us, so that it would be inappropriate to say that an idea "belonged" to any one person; the idea becomes enlarged and transformed in interchange so that it is not what it was when it began and it is truly everyone's creation. On other points, we do not all think alike and we keep struggling to honor these differences and to learn from them.

Some of the comments included in the foreword to the original edition of this book should be requoted here. I noted there that I cited experiences from certain women's lives and that these descriptions are simplified and schematic. They are used as illustrations only. For the protection of the people involved they are heavily disguised. These vignettes do not begin to reproduce the vividness and complexity of a person's real experience.

I have not attempted to deal with the class and racial factors which make an enormous difference in women's lives.

Foreword

I have not discussed lesbian women. I believe that other writers can speak on these topics with greater knowledge. In general, I have concentrated on the factors which I believed existed for all women, by virtue of being women.

I discussed portions of the material with several individuals and groups of people who gave far more than the usual time and attention to comments and criticism. Further, Pearl and Roy Bennett, Anne Bernays, Barbara DuBois, and Joan Zilbach read and closely critiqued, often on short notice, all or large portions of earlier versions of the manuscript.

I should like to express appreciation also to the *American Journal of Orthopsychiatry* for permission to use material first published there in a different version.

The fact that this book exists as a book is due to MaryAnn Lash, who was Associate Director and later Director of Beacon Press at the time of the first edition of this book. She taught me that a book can be part of a process. (I thought I had that idea about other things but could not extend it to a book.) Not only can a book be part of a process, but the making of this book had been a new process of bookmaking for us. At each stage along the way the material went back and forth between us, with MaryAnn continuing to make a major contribution to it. No small part of that contribution was her ability to pierce through to make something coherent out of an impenetrable prose that would surely have defeated a lesser mind and discouraged a less devoted person. She had that great and rare gift: the ability to evoke and enhance while never intruding or violating. If only we could all do this for each other! This ability was a demonstration in action of the things I was trying to write about. Joanne Wyckoff, Senior Editor at Beacon Press, has carried out this tradition for the second edition. I am extremely grateful to her.

Final decisions were always mine and therefore final responsibility is too.

Foreword

Most of all I want to thank my husband, Mike, and my sons, Jon and Ned, for all their help and fun and love. I have learned a great deal from each of them and each is in his different way a new kind of man. I have had rare good fortune.

J.B.M.

July 1986
Boston, Massachusetts

toward a new psychology of women

part i   the makings of the mind
 – so far

Humanity has been held to a limited and distorted view of itself — from its interpretation of the most intimate of personal emotions to its grandest vision of human possibilities — precisely by virtue of its subordination of women.

Until recently, "mankind's" understandings have been the only understandings generally available to us. As other perceptions arise — precisely those perceptions that men, because of their dominant position, could not perceive — the total vision of human possibilities enlarges and is transformed. The old is severely challenged.

Women have been in a subservient position, in many ways like that of a subservient class or caste. Thus it is necessary to look first at women as "unequals" or subordinates. But it is immediately apparent, too, that women's position cannot be understood solely in terms of inequality. An even more complex dynamic follows.

Women have played a specific role in male-led society in ways no other suppressed groups have done. They have been entwined with men in intimate and intense relationships, creating the milieu — the family — in which the human mind as we know it has been formed. Thus women's situation is a crucial key to understanding the psychological order.

chapter one

domination–
subordination

Throughout this book we will struggle with the issue of difference: what do people do to people who are different from them and why? On the individual level, the child grows only via engagement with people very different from her/himself. Thus, the most significant difference is between the adult and the child. At the level of humanity in general, we have seen massive problems around a great variety of differences. But the most basic difference is the one between women and men.

On both levels it is appropriate to pose two questions. When does the engagement of difference stimulate the development and the enhancement of both parties to the engagement? And, conversely, when does such a confrontation with difference have negative effects: when does it lead to great difficulty, deterioration, and distortion and to some of the worst forms of degradation, terror, and violence — both for individuals and for groups — that human beings can experience? It is clear that "mankind" in general, especially in our Western tradition but in some others as well, does not have a very glorious record in this regard.

It is not always clear that in most instances of difference there is also a factor of inequality — inequality of many kinds of resources, but fundamentally of status and power. One useful way to examine the often confusing results of these confrontations with difference is to ask: What happens in situations of

3

inequality? What forces are set in motion? While we will be using the terms "dominant" and "subordinate" in the discussion, it is useful to remember that flesh and blood women and men are involved. Speaking in abstractions sometimes permits us to accept what we might not admit to on a personal level.

Temporary Inequality

Two types of inequality are pertinent for present purposes. The first might be called temporary inequality. Here, the lesser party is *socially* defined as unequal. Major examples are the relationships between parents and children, teachers and students, and, possibly, therapists and clients. There are certain assumptions in these relationships which are often not made explicit, nor, in fact, are they carried through. But they are the social structuring of the relationship.

The "superior" party presumably has more of some ability or valuable quality, which she/he is supposed to impart to the "lesser" person. While these abilities vary with the particular relationship, they include emotional maturity, experience in the world, physical skills, a body of knowledge, or the techniques for acquiring certain kinds of knowledge. The superior person is supposed to engage with the lesser in such a way as to bring the lesser member up to full parity; that is, the child is to be helped to become the adult. Such is the overall task of this relationship. The lesser, the child, is to be given to, by the person who presumably has more to give. Although the lesser party often also gives much to the superior, these relationships are *based in service* to the lesser party. That is their *raison d'être*.

It is clear, then, that the paramount goal is to end the relationship; that is, to end the relationship of inequality. The period of disparity is meant to be temporary. People may continue their association as friends, colleagues, or even competitors, but not as "superior" and "lesser." At least this is the goal.

The reality is that we have trouble enough with this sort of relationship. Parents or professional institutions often tip toward serving the needs of the donor instead of those of the lesser party (for example, schools can come to serve teachers or administrators, rather than students). Or the lesser person learns how to be a good "lesser" rather than how to make the journey from lesser to full stature. Overall, we have not found very good ways to carry out the central task: to foster the movement from unequal to equal. In childrearing and education we do not have an adequate theory and practice. Nor do we have concepts that work well in such other unequal so-called "helping" relationships as healing, penology, and rehabilitation. Officially, we say we want to do these things, but we often fail.

We have a great deal of trouble deciding on how many rights "to allow" to the lesser party. We agonize about how much power the lesser party shall have. How much can the lesser person express or act on her or his perceptions when these definitely differ from those of the superior? Above all, there is great difficulty in maintaining the conception of the lesser person *as a person of as much intrinsic worth as the superior.*

A crucial point is that power is a major factor in all of these relationships. But power alone will not suffice. Power exists and it has to be taken into account, not denied. The superiors hold all the real power, but power will not accomplish *the task.* It will not bring the unequal party up to equality.

Our troubles with these relationships may stem from the fact that they exist within the context of a second type of inequality that tends to overwhelm the ways we learn to operate in the first kind. The second type molds the very ways we perceive and conceptualize what we are doing in the first, most basic kind of relationships.

The second type of inequality teaches us how to enforce inequality, but not how to make the journey from unequal to equal. Most importantly, its consequences are kept amazingly obscure — in fact they are usually denied. In this book we will concentrate on this second kind of inequality. However, the underlying notion is that this second type has determined, and still determines, the only ways we can think and feel in the first type.

Permanent Inequality

In these relationships, some people or groups of people are defined as unequal by means of what sociologists call ascription; that is, your birth defines you. Criteria may be race, sex, class, nationality, religion, or other characteristics ascribed at birth.[1] Here, the terms of the relationship are very different from those of temporary inequality. There is, for example, no notion that superiors are present primarily to help inferiors, to impart to them their advantages and "desirable" characteristics. There is no assumption that the goal of the unequal relationship is to end the inequality; in fact, quite the reverse. A series of other governing tendencies are in force, and occur with a great regularity. I shall suggest some of these tendencies first on a superficial level; we will then come back to them, to show how they operate at a much more intense, subtle, and profound personal level. While some of these elements may appear obvious, in fact there is a great deal of disagreement and confusion about psychological characteristics brought about by conditions as obvious as these.

Dominants. Once a group is defined as inferior, the superiors tend to label it as defective or substandard in various ways. These labels accrete rapidly. Thus, blacks are described as less intelligent than whites, women are supposed to be ruled by emotion, and so on. In addition, the actions and words of the dominant group tend to be destructive of the subordinates. All historical evidence confirms this tendency. And, although they are much less obvious, there are destructive effects on the dominants as well. The latter are of a different order and are much more difficult to recognize; they will be discussed further in this and in subsequent chapters.

Dominant groups usually define one or more acceptable roles for the subordinate. Acceptable roles typically involve providing services that no dominant group wants to perform for itself (for example, cleaning up the dominant's waste products). Functions that a dominant group prefers to perform, on the other hand, are carefully guarded and closed to subordinates. Out of the total range of human possibilities, the activities most highly valued in any particular culture will tend to be enclosed within the domain of the dominant group; less valued functions are relegated to the subordinates.

Subordinates are usually said to be unable to perform the preferred roles. Their incapacities are ascribed to innate defects or deficiencies of mind or body, therefore immutable and impossible of change or development. It becomes difficult for dominants even to imagine that subordinates are capable of performing the preferred activities. More importantly, subordinates themselves can come to find it difficult to believe in their own ability. The myth of their inability to fulfill wider or more valued roles is challenged only when a drastic event disrupts the usual arrangements. Such disruptions usually arise from outside the relationship itself. For instance, in the emergency situation of World War II, "incompetent" women suddenly "manned" the factories with great skill.

It follows that subordinates are described in terms of, and encouraged to develop, personal psychological characteristics that are pleasing to the dominant group. These characteristics form a certain familiar cluster: submissiveness, passivity, docility, dependency, lack of initiative, inability to act, to decide, to think, and the like. In general, this cluster includes qualities more characteristic of children than adults — immaturity, weakness, and helplessness. If subordinates adopt these characteristics they are considered well-adjusted.

However, when subordinates show the potential for, or even more dangerously have developed other characteristics — let us say intelligence, initiative, assertiveness — there is usually no room available within the dominant framework for acknowledgement of these characteristics. Such people will be defined as at least unusual, if not definitely abnormal. There will be no opportunities for the direct application of their abilities within the social arrangements. (How many women have pretended to be dumb!)

Dominant groups usually impede the development of subordinates and block their freedom of expression and action. They also tend to militate against stirrings of greater rationality or greater humanity in their own members. It was not too long ago that "nigger lover" was a common appellation, and even now men who "allow their women" more than the usual scope are subject to ridicule in many circles.

A dominant group, inevitably, has the greatest influence in determining a culture's overall outlook — its philosophy, morality, social theory, and even its science. The dominant group, thus, legitimizes the unequal relationship and incorporates it into society's guiding concepts. The social outlook, then, obscures the true nature of this relationship — that is, the very existence of inequality. The culture explains the events that take place in terms of other premises, premises that are inevitably false, such as racial or sexual inferiority. While in recent years we have learned about many such falsities on the larger social level, a full analysis of the psychological implications still remains to be developed. In the case of women, for example, despite overwhelming evidence to the contrary, the notion persists that women are meant to be passive, submissive, docile, secondary. From this premise, the outcome of therapy and encounters with psychology and other "sciences" are often determined.

Inevitably, the dominant group is the model for "normal human relationships." It then becomes "normal" to treat others destructively and to derogate them, to obscure the truth of what you are doing, by creating false explanations, and to oppose actions toward equality. In short, if one's identification is with the dominant group, it is "normal" to continue in this pattern. Even though most of us do not like to think of ourselves as either believing in, or engaging in, such domination, it is, in fact, difficult for a member of a dominant group to do otherwise. But to keep on doing these things, one need only behave "normally."

It follows from this that dominant groups generally do not like to be told about or even quietly reminded of the existence of inequality. "Normally" they can avoid awareness because their explanation of the relationship becomes so well integrated *in other terms*; they can even believe that both they and the subordinate group share the same interests and, to some extent, a common experience. If pressed a bit, the familiar rationalizations are offered: the home is "women's natural place," and we know "what's best for them anyhow."

Dominants prefer to avoid conflict — open conflict that might call into question the whole situation. This is particularly and tragically so, when many members of the dominant group are not having an easy time of it themselves. Members of a dominant group, or at least some segments of it, such as white working-class men (who are themselves also subordinates), often feel unsure of their own narrow toehold on the material and psychological bounties they believe they desperately need. What dominant groups usually cannot act on, or even see, is that the situation of inequality in fact deprives them, particularly on the psychological level.

Clearly, inequality has created a state of conflict. Yet dominant groups will tend to suppress conflict. They will see any questioning of the "normal" situation as threatening; activities by subordinates in this direction will be perceived with alarm. Dominants are usually convinced that the way things are is right and good, not only for them but especially for the subordinates. All morality confirms this view, and all social structure sustains it.

It is perhaps unnecessary to add that the dominant group usually holds all of the open power and authority and determines the ways in which power may be acceptably used.

Subordinates. What of the subordinates' part in this? Since dominants determine what is normal for a culture, it is much more difficult to understand subordinates. Initial expressions of dissatisfaction and early actions by subordinates always come as a surprise; they are usually rejected as atypical. After all, dominants *knew* that all women needed and wanted was a man around whom to organize their lives. Members of the dominant group do not understand why "they" — the first to speak out — are so upset and angry.

The characteristics that typify the subordinates are even more complex. A subordinate group has to concentrate on basic survival. Accordingly, direct, honest reaction to destructive treatment is avoided. Open, self-initiated action in its own self-interest must also be avoided. Such actions can, and still do, literally result in death for some subordinate groups. In our own society, a woman's direct action can result in a combination of economic hardship, social ostracism, and psychological isolation — and even the diagnosis of a personality disorder. Any one of these consequences is bad enough. Some examples of them and how they are used to control women's behavior will be discussed in subsequent chapters.

It is not surprising then that a subordinate group resorts to disguised and indirect ways of acting and reacting. While these actions are designed to accommodate and please the dominant group, they often, in fact, contain hidden defiance and "put ons." Folk tales, black jokes, and women stories are often based on how the wily peasant or sharecropper outwitted the rich landowner, boss, or husband. The essence of the story rests on the fact that the overlord does not even know that he has been made a fool of.

One important result of this indirect mode of operation is that members of the dominant group are denied an essential part of life — the opportunity to acquire self-understanding through knowing their impact on others. They are thus deprived of "consensual validation," feedback, and a chance to correct their actions and expressions. Put simply, subordinates won't tell. For the same reasons, the dominant group is deprived also of valid knowledge about the subordinates. (It is particularly ironic that the societal "experts" in knowledge about subordinates are usually members of the dominant group.)

Subordinates, then, know much more about the dominants than vice versa. They have to. They become highly attuned to the dominants, able to predict their reactions of pleasure and displeasure. Here, I think, is where the long story of "feminine intuition" and "feminine wiles" begins. It seems clear that these "mysterious" gifts are in fact skills, developed through long practice, in reading many small signals, both verbal and nonverbal.

Another important result is that subordinates often know more about the dominants than they know about themselves. If a large part of your fate depends on accommodating to and pleasing the dominants, you concentrate on them. Indeed, there is little purpose in knowing yourself. Why should you when your knowledge of the dominants determines your life? This tendency is reinforced by many other restrictions. One can know oneself only through action and interaction. To the extent that their range of action or interaction is limited, subordinates will lack a realistic evaluation of their capacities and problems. Unfortunately, this difficulty in gaining self-knowledge is even further compounded.

Tragic confusion arises because subordinates absorb a large part of the untruths created by the dominants; there are a great many blacks who feel inferior to whites, and women who still believe they are less important than men. This internalization of dominant beliefs is more likely to occur if there are few alternative concepts at hand. On the other hand, it is also true that members of the subordinate group have certain experiences and perceptions that accurately reflect the truth about themselves and the injustice of their position. Their own more truthful concepts are bound to come into opposition with the mythology they have absorbed from the dominant group. An inner tension between the two sets of concepts and their derivatives is almost inevitable.

From a historical perspective, despite the obstacles, subordinate groups have tended to move toward greater freedom of expression and action, although this progress varies greatly from one circumstance to another. There were always some slaves who revolted; there were some women who sought greater development or self-determination. Most records of these actions are not preserved by the dominant culture, making it difficult for the subordinate group to find a supporting tradition and history.

Within each subordinate group, there are tendencies for some members to imitate the dominants. This imitation can take various forms. Some may try to treat their fellow subordinates as destructively as the dominants treat them. A few may develop enough of the qualities valued by the dominants to be partially accepted into their fellowship. Usually they are not wholly accepted, and even then only if they are willing to forsake their own identification with fellow subordinates. "Uncle

Toms" and certain professional women have often been in this position. (There are always a few women who have won the praise presumably embodied in the phrase "she thinks like a man.")

To the extent that subordinates move toward freer expression and action, they will expose the inequality and throw into question the basis for its existence. And they will make the inherent conflict an open conflict. They will then have to bear the burden and take the risks that go with being defined as "troublemakers." Since this role flies in the face of their conditioning, subordinates, especially women, do not come to it with ease.

What is immediately apparent from studying the characteristics of the two groups is that mutually enhancing interaction is not probable between unequals. Indeed, conflict is inevitable. The important questions, then, become: Who defines the conflict? Who sets the terms? When is conflict overt or covert? On what issues is the conflict fought? Can anyone win? Is conflict "bad," by definition? If not, what makes for productive or destructive conflict?

chapter two

conflict — the old way

Covert Conflict — Closed Conflict

Conflict, seen in its fullest sense, is not necessarily threatening or destructive. Quite the contrary. We shall try to develop an enlarged view of the many dimensions of conflict as we go along, but for the moment we can say that we all grow via conflict. On the individual level, the infant would never grow if it interacted with a mirror image of itself. Growth requires engagement with difference and with people embodying that difference. If differences were more openly acknowledged, we could allow for, and even encourage, an increasingly strong expression by each party of her or his experience. This would lead to greater clarity for self, greater ability to fulfill one's own needs, and more facility to respond to others. There would be a chance at individual and mutual satisfaction, growth, and even joy.

Within a framework of inequality the existence of conflict is denied and the means to engage openly in conflict are excluded. Further, inequality itself creates additional factors that skew any interaction and prevent open engagement around real differences. Instead, inequality generates hidden conflict around elements that the inequality itself has set in motion. In sum, both sides are diverted from open conflict around real differences, by which they could grow, and are channeled into hidden conflict around falsifications. For this hidden conflict, there are no acceptable social forms or guides because this conflict supposedly doesn't exist.

Finally, there is massive misunderstanding about the qualities and characteristics of each of the parties to the conflict. One can try to cut through this complicated situation by asking: what *actually* happens in the male-female conflict situation today?

In a situation of male-female inequality, there are two possible scenarios. The nature of conflict seems to hinge on the degree to which the woman does or does not accept the man's conception about herself. If she accepts his outlook, she will not recognize that there is a conflict of interests or needs. Instead, she will assume implicitly that her needs will be fulfilled if she accepts a position generally oriented around the primacy of men and service to their needs. Sometimes this assumption "works," depending on various sets of circumstances and considerable luck.

Paradoxically, it seems to work best when women are to a large degree conscious of what they are doing — if they are really moving out of this model, but keeping up the pretense that they are not. They cater to the picture of the superior importance and claims of men. At the same time, they have developed enough sense of their own rights and abilities and enough recognition of their own needs to act on them; and they do manage to get them fulfilled to some extent. This is the style of the so-called "smart woman" that, stretched to absurdity, dominated so many television family situation comedies in the last decade. The clever wife manages to get what she wants by somehow making it seem that this is what her husband wants. All the while, the poor husband doesn't really know what's happening. Or, if he does, he does not "let on." Combined with an appreciation of her cleverness is an implied criticism that women are naturally "tricky."

These relationships are not based on increasing openness and mutual understanding; they contain a large element of deception and manipulation; there is often quite obvious reciprocal condescension. Such relationships, although not the best bases for mutual growth, often "work," at least for a while; and certain of them may even allow leeway for fulfillment of some needs for each partner. The woman is usually highly skillful; the most effective are careful not to let on how skillful they really are.

Much deeper trouble occurs when subordinates incorporate the dominant group's conception of themselves as inferior or secondary. Such women are less able to recognize and clarify their own needs, either to themselves or to the men. Instead, they believe the man will somehow fulfill these needs and then are disappointed, often very miserably. This situation can lead to a series of escalating demands that the man fulfill needs that are increasingly unclear and may even become inappropriate and excessive.

The example of one family may illustrate this point. I will recount the stark outlines of a long story as both wife and husband came to see it after much anguish. It is the kind of situation many psychiatrists, novelists, and playwrights refer to frequently because, in a curious way, it seems to be a picture of the strong woman. (The material is presented first in rather cursory fashion and then with greater analysis.)

From the beginning, Sally, the wife, accepted her place as subordinate. While she did not openly complain, she began to mention fairly often the many things she felt were missing — the lack of time together as a family, the limitations of the budget, the vacations they did not take. She made clear, without ever fully verbalizing it, her feelings that her husband, Don, was less able than she had believed him to be, less successful, less adequate than other men. She began to emphasize his relative unimportance within the home and to indicate that his failure to find sufficient time for his family must have been the result of his inefficiency. Meanwhile, she displayed her qualities as a worker, demonstrating the speed and ability with which she cared for her home. She spent a great deal of time with her two children and believed this indicated her greater devotion and "love." As the problems deepened, she emphasized increasingly her husband's weaknesses. Don tended, for example, to make impulsive decisions, which he himself sometimes regretted. He could no longer discuss this problem within the relationship because Sally now magnified his errors and believed that they were a major cause of family problems.

By contrasting her own, more sober reflections, she established her superiority. Don became less and less able to defend himself against this psychological sabotage since each charge contained some grain of truth. Sally used his weaknesses to downgrade him and to treat him with contempt. In time, he came to feel inadequate and unsuccessful, less "manly," humiliated, and demeaned. His children, too, began to regard him as weak, less knowing, less masterful, and less concerned than their mother. They looked to her to fulfill their needs. At the same time they hated and distrusted her, blaming her for the destruction of their father.

Sally and Don had waged a devastatingly deceptive, covert campaign, but had gained no victories. Sally certainly did not have the competent husband she thought she wanted. At the same time, she was afraid to go out in the world to accomplish anything herself. Indeed, she was ill-prepared to do so, having earlier surrendered her opportunities for education or work experience in order to advance her husband's. During the course of the campaign, she also had lost much: she too had been neglected and diminished.

Sally was not asking openly for equality. She didn't think in such terms. She was not struggling to develop her capacities or interests. If she had, she would have run into conflict with her husband and with educational and economic institutions much earlier. Her conflict was of a very different nature. Though she would have been called a troublemaker if she had sought, and certainly if she had demanded, no less than an equal chance to explore her own needs and interests, she would have been on different ground. Instead, her perceptions of her needs were distorted and her demands took the form of criticism of her husband's adequacy. The implicit message of her behavior was that Don "was not being enough of a man." Since both husband and wife were caught up in this dynamic, there was a mounting attack on, and diminution of, the man's "manliness." This, combined with anger over, and punishment for, unmet needs, turned the model into exactly what men think they fear most: the man is made to feel inferior to the woman. It is not that the situation of inequality has been changed, but that positions within the model *seem* to be reversed.

In fact, the model that women are encouraged to adopt has been that of so-called "temporary inequality," which we have described above. Men — the superiors — are said to be "more" or to "have more." Such a model is obviously inappropriate between two adults, for it leads to covert expectations and demands that can undermine the man's psychological resources. There should have been an open attack on his position of dominance and greater privilege. This would have been ultimately beneficial to the man as well as to the woman. But women are strongly discouraged from initiating that kind of struggle.

Moreover, the dominant ethic often induces women to view themselves and their own attempts to know, and act on their needs — or to enlarge their lives beyond the prescribed bounds — as either attacking men or trying to be like them. At bottom, women believe they must be destructive if they attempt it. Indeed, efforts by women to enrich their lives, even in the direction of their own traditionally feminine concerns, were, and still are, readily misinterpreted as attempts to diminish or imitate men. It has been very difficult for women themselves to perceive self-development in any other terms.

Overt Conflict — Open-Ended Conflict

If subordinates do not accept their place as inferior or secondary, they will initiate open conflict. That is, if women assume that their own needs have equal validity and proceed to explore and state them more openly, they will be seen as creating conflict and must bear the psychological burden of rejecting men's images of "true womanhood." This can lead to discomfort, anxiety, and even more serious reactions for both parties. The hope, however, is that interaction between two resourceful and competent adults can bring the needs of both people closer to fulfillment. Both men and women will cease laboring under demands that are not fully known or recognized and that are doomed to go unmet. (The particular covert and overt demands under which women labor will be treated much more extensively throughout the rest of this book.)

In order to understand the unnecessarily destructive situation in Sally and Don's family, it is necessary to describe them in a little more detail. Both had reached adulthood with many resources and with possibilities for further development. Both had a number of problems of a fairly similar sort, but they handled their basic problems in different ways. They had some fairly strong doubts about their abilities to exist and function safely as separate individuals. Both longed in some measure for the strong, all-caring person who would provide solutions to their problems; they were also prepared to rage against that person. Yet, each had capacities upon which she or he could have built a greater individual sense of strength and safety.

Initially, Sally saw in Don's carefreeness, humor, slight daring, and seeming lack of concern a much-longed-for path out of her own hated feelings of inadequacy and inability to act freely and yet safely; she admired the very things she later condemned so harshly. Don, for his part, saw in his wife's steadiness and efficiency some of the strengths and securities for which he longed. Each could have "learned" much from the partner's way of handling these basic issues, but this does not usually happen when a relationship fails to allow for and respond to important needs.

In a situation of inequality the woman is not encouraged to take her own needs seriously, to explore them, to try to act on them as a full-fledged person. She is enjoined from engaging all of her own resources and thereby prevented from developing some valid and reliable sense of her own worth. Instead, the woman is encouraged to concentrate on the needs and development of the man.

To concentrate on and to take seriously one's own development is hard enough for all human beings. But, as has been recently demonstrated in many areas, it has been even harder for women. Women are not encouraged to develop as far as they possibly can and to experience the stimulation and the anguish, anxiety, and pain the process entails. Instead, they are encouraged to concentrate on forming and maintaining a relationship to one person. In fact, women are encouraged to believe that if they do go through the mental and emotional struggle of self-development, the end result will be disastrous — they will forfeit the possibility of having any close relationships. This penalty, this threat of isolation, is intolerable for anyone to contemplate. For women, reality has made the threat; it was by no means imaginary.

To avoid this outcome, women are encouraged to do two things. First, they are diverted from exploring and expressing their needs (which would threaten terrible isolation or severe conflict not only with men but with all our institutions as they are arranged and, equally importantly, with their inner image of what it means to be a woman). Secondly, women are encouraged to "transform" their own needs. This often means that they fail, automatically and without perceiving it, to recognize their own needs as such. They come to see their needs as if they were identical to those of others — usually men or children. If women can manage this transformation and can fulfill the perceived needs of others, then, they believe, they will feel comfortable and fulfilled. Women who can do so will seemingly be most comfortable with social arrangements as they now are. The trouble is that this is a most precarious transformation; it hangs by a delicate thread, and I have seen many people, who, it could be said, have broken this thread.

An example of this transformation carried to the extreme is suggested in the studies of families of people suffering from severe psychological trouble — the so-called schizophrenics. In these families, the parents, particularly the mother, seem to perceive their own conflicted and unresolved needs as somehow those of the child. These studies lead one to suspect that such families are not idiosyncratic occurrences, but rather intensified examples of a situation that exists for all.

Thus, it may be no accident that in the years preceding the current reexamination of women's position, it was reported in psychiatric literature that one after another major psychological situation was "caused" by the "dominating mother" and the "weak, ineffectual father." This was said to be true of schizophrenia, homosexuality, delinquency, alienated youth, and practically every other psychological or social topic. To the extent that such observations were valid, they probably reflected the pressure of the conflicting needs of both men and women. They were probably especially indicative of the fact that women are encouraged both to seek the fulfillment of all their needs in the family and also to *transform* these needs — to try to believe that their needs belong, not to them but to someone else.

All of this will be unraveled and explored further in subsequent chapters. First, I would like to approach our tragic situation from another vantage point.

chapter three

the importance of unimportant people

We have seen that as a society emphasizes and values some aspects of the total range of human potentials more than others, the valued aspects are associated closely with, and limited to, the dominant group's domain. Certain other elements are relegated to subordinates. Although these may be necessary parts of human experience, they are not the ones valued by that particular society. Furthermore, subordinates cannot easily call attention to this distribution.

Several black writers have described this experience. They have said that as American society, in the larger tradition of Western society, has valued the intellect and the executive and managerial functions, physical labor has been relegated to the domain of blacks and lower-class whites. At the same time, people who do manual labor have often been seen as less manageable members of society. Thus, we have had the myth of the sexual prowess of the black as well as the idea that the trucker or hard hat is a rough, tough customer. One can see the same process in operation in another form vis-à-vis women because the realm of biology — the body, sex, and childbearing — are hers. Primary interaction with children, and childish things, is also relegated to women.

I mentioned earlier that subordinates are assigned generally less-valued tasks. It is interesting to note that these tasks usually involve providing bodily needs and comforts. Subordinates are expected to make pleasant, orderly, or clean those parts of the body or things to do with the body that are perceived as unpleasant, uncontrollable, or dirty. (Providing clean laundry is one superficial example; providing a necessary sexual outlet is another, not so superficial, example.)

It seems possible that Freud had to discover the very specialized technique of psychoanalysis because there were crucial parts of the human experience that were not well provided for in fully acceptable and socially open ways within the culture of the dominant group. That is, they were not well provided for by the dominants *for* the dominants *themselves*. These same realms of experience have been consistently relegated to women.

What has psychoanalysis really been dealing with? First, Freud focused on bodily, sexual, and childish experience and said that these are of determining but hidden importance. More recent psychoanalytic theory tends to emphasize the deeper issues of feelings of vulnerability, weakness, helplessness, dependency, and the basic emotional connections between an individual and other people. That is, psychoanalysis has in a very large sense been engaged in bringing about the acknowledgment of these crucial realms of the human experience. It has done this, I think, without recognizing that these areas of experience may have been kept out of people's conscious awareness by virtue of their being so heavily dissociated from men and so heavily associated with women. It is not that men, like all people, do not have experience in these areas. As psychoanalysis has been engaged in pointing out, these are most significant human experiences. Indeed, they involve the necessities of human experience. One might even say that we came to "need" psychoanalysis precisely because certain essential parts of men's experience have been very problematic and therefore were unacknowledged, unexplored, and denied.

Women, then, become the "carriers" for society of certain aspects of the total human experience — those aspects that remain unsolved. (This is one reason why women must be so mistreated and degraded.) The result of such a process is to keep men from fully integrating these areas into their own lives. These parts of experience have been removed from the arena of full and open interchange and relegated increasingly to a realm outside of full awareness, in which they take on all sorts of frightening attributes. Because women have been less able than men to express their own experiences and concerns, they have not been able to reintroduce these elements into the normal social exchange.

We have said that our cultural tradition has emphasized certain human potentials and seen these as very important. Whatever their origin, these abilities became highly valued and were elaborated by the dominant culture. They had to be painstakingly cultivated; tendencies that interfered with them had to be put aside and tamed or "mastered."

The aspects that it seemed most necessary to master would be those perceived as uncontrollable or as evidence of weakness and helplessness. Learning to master passion and weakness became a major task of growing up as a man. But sexuality, precisely because of its insistence and its intense pleasure, can become an area of threat, something that undermines carefully developed controls. Equally threatening is the realm of "object relations" — that is, the intense involvement with other people of both sexes. In fact, men are strongly pulled both toward other people sexually and in a more total emotional sense; but they have also erected strong barriers against this pull. And here, I think, is the greatest source of fear: the totally false belief that the pull will reduce them to some undifferentiated mass or state ruled by weakness, emotional attachment, and/or passion and that they will thereby lose the long-sought and fought-for status of manhood. This threat, I believe, is the deeper one that equality poses, for it is perceived erroneously not as equality only but as a total stripping of the person.

Much of current literature, philosophy, and social commentary focuses on the lack of human connection in all our institutions. There is widespread concern about our inability to organize the fruits of technology toward human ends; it is, perhaps, the central problem of the dominant culture. But human ends have been traditionally assigned to women; indeed, women's lives have been principally occupied with them. When women have raised questions that reflect their concerns, the issues have been pushed aside and labeled trivial matters. In fact, now as in the past, the issues are anything but trivial; rather, they are the highly charged, unsolved problems of the dominant culture as a whole, and they are laden with dreaded associations. The charge of triviality is more likely massively defensive, for the questions threaten the return of what has been warded off, denied, and sealed away — under the label "female."

To put this point another way, we might ask, "In the current resurgence of the women's movement, what are the issues that have emerged?" Are they not, in many instances, expressions of the fact that women are the bearers of these human necessities for the social group as a whole? What have women, at long last openly, "complained" about and received the most criticism for complaining about? Here, the more radical spokeswomen have emphasized the objectives most clearly:

1. Physical Frankness — Open talk about one's body — in order to know about it and how it works — has as its goal being in touch with one's body, rather than controlling it or claiming that it controls you. There is also a firm rejection of all forms of outside control of women's bodies, ranging from direct sexual control to legislative fiat.

2. Sexual Frankness — Open knowledge about sexual matters is a pressing need, as is a redefinition of female sexuality in women's terms rather than as it is perceived by men. An important aspect of this objective is the elimination of the role of sexual object and a greater emphasis on the connection among sexual, personal, and emotional meanings.

3. Emotional Frankness — Open expression of the emotions involved in all experience, especially those not encouraged by the dominant culture, is essential to psychological health. At the same time, women want to express openly their sense of power, something they have certainly not been encouraged to do.

4. Human Development — Responsibility for the care and fostering of human development has traditionally been discussed in terms of children and who should care for them. It is now a larger question of how we, as people, shall provide for proper care and growth of *all* people, children and adults. This includes redistribution of responsibility for what have been called "services" for others. Such "services" are often bodily related (such as brewing the office coffee), but extend to questions of providing for others in very basic and essential psychological ways.

5. Objectification — Many women have strongly protested against objectification, not only in sexual but in all ways. They are no longer willing to be treated as if they were "things" throughout every level of life.

6. Private and Public Equality — Demands for equal, mutual, and more cooperative living to replace the dominance-oriented, competitive styles prevalent in both public and private spheres are growing. There is challenge across the board of hierarchy, control, and "distancing" of people.

7. Personal Creativity — Especially important is the right to participate in creating one's own personhood, as opposed to accepting the form and content prescribed for you by the dominant group.

This list of issues suggests a most interesting and exciting proposition: in the course of projecting into women's domain some of its most troublesome and problematic exigencies, male-led society may also have simultaneously, and unwittingly, delegated to women not humanity's "lowest needs" but its "highest necessities" — that is, the intense, emotionally connected cooperation and creativity necessary for human life and growth. Further, it is women who today perceive that they must openly and consciously demand them if they are to achieve even the beginnings of personal integrity.

In many ways women have "filled in" these essentials all along. Precisely because they have done so, women have developed the foundations of extremely valuable psychological qualities, which we are only beginning to understand. I hope that soon knowledge gained from several areas of study will help us to delineate these strengths and their dynamic operation in richer and more precise terms. In the next part, I should like to briefly describe some of these psychological characteristics as seen in experience in psychotherapy.

Also in that part I will suggest that while psychoanalysis has passed through two historical stages in terms of major content, the issues raised in the list of women's current concerns may point to a "third stage," one that psychoanalysis itself has not yet defined. A shorthand way of putting it may be to say that psychoanalysis has been doing "women's work," but it has not recognized it for what it was. It had to undertake "women's work" in the first place because the dominant culture did not do this work nor take it into consideration. Therein lie its problems.

part ii   *looking in both directions*

*Beyond inequality, women have a further, more complex
relation to male society. Women have not only been treated as
unequals — in many ways like other groups of people socially
defined as subordinate — but they have been sustaining a
special, more total dynamic.*

*It is most important to emphasize that the psychological
characteristics to be discussed in this section are in all instances two-sided. They are qualities that are presently more
highly developed in women as a group. In a situation of
inequality and powerlessness, these characteristics can lead to
subservience and to complex psychological problems, as we
shall try to demonstrate. On the other hand, the dialogue is
always with the future. These same characteristics represent
potentials that can provide a new framework, one which
would have to be inevitably different from that of the dominant male society. Bernard S. Robbins first advanced the idea
that women's psychological characteristics are closer to certain
psychological essentials and are, therefore, both sources of
strength and the bases of a more advanced form of living.[1]*

*I have labeled these characteristics "strengths" because this
is a point I wish to emphasize. They have been called "weaknesses" and even women, themselves, have so interpreted them.*

27

That very designation has been part of the devaluation and obscurantism associated with them.

The topics covered in this part bear a certain suggestive correspondence to the issues of central concern in the current stage of psychoanalytic thought. Psychoanalysts today find themselves occupied with the origins and nature of the individual's most basic sense of connection with other human beings. Major concerns are the so-called "dependency needs" (a phrase to be debated), the development of autonomy and/or independence, and the issues of basic feelings of weakness and vulnerability. (Otto Kernberg and Heinz Kohut, for example, are two of the current psychoanalytic writers in this area. Among others have been Karen Horney, Harry S. Sullivan, Frieda Fromm-Reichmann, and W. D. R. Fairbairn.) I will not attempt to spell out this correspondence in detail, nor discuss these subjects in the usual psychoanalytic terms, but will merely suggest that all of these issues are intimately related to, and associated with, the position assigned to women in our social and psychological structuring of life. Indeed, I believe the very terms in which we conceptualize these issues reflect their origins in the situation in which women have played a key, but submerged, role. In the next chapter we will show that women's attempts to deal with these issues lead into the heart of what may be the next, and not yet defined, stage for psychoanalysis or psychological theory.

The effort here is to look at the complexities of psychological theory from what is, in fact, a totally different vantage point — that which begins with a consideration of some of women's characteristics. We will start this examination on a simple descriptive level and then return to recapitulate some of the complications that follow. When we have accomplished that, we may be in a position to better understand the dynamics that operate to create and maintain the present situation — or, alternatively, to change it.

chapter four

strengths

Vulnerability, Weakness, Helplessness

Today in psychotherapy a central place is given to feelings of weakness, vulnerability, and helplessness, along with their usual accompaniment, feelings of neediness. These are feelings we have all known, given the long period necessary for maturational development in human beings and, in our society, given the difficulties and lack of support most of us suffer during childhood and indeed in our adult lives. Such feelings are, of course, most unpleasant — in their extreme, they are terrifying — and several schools of psychodynamic thought postulate that they are the root causes of various major "pathologies." In Western society men are encouraged to dread, abhor, or deny feeling weak or helpless, whereas women are encouraged to cultivate this state of being. The first and most important point, however, is that these feelings are common and inevitable to all, even though our cultural tradition unrealistically expects men to discard rather than to acknowledge them.

Two brief examples illustrate this contrast. Mary, a gifted and resourceful young hospital worker with two children, was offered a new and more demanding position. She would lead a team attempting an innovative approach to patient care. It involved greater scope for the team members and for Mary a harder job of coordination and negotiation of the workers' anxieties and difficulties. Mary's immediate reaction was to worry about her ability to carry out the project; she felt weak and helpless in the face of the formidable task. At times, she was convinced she was totally incapable of doing the job and wanted to refuse the offer.

Her worry was in some measure appropriate, for the position of team coordinator was a difficult and demanding one that should be approached only after rigorous self-evaluation. She was, however, extremely able and had demonstrated the abilities necessary for the position. She retained some common feminine problems — having trouble admitting to, and easily losing sight of, her strengths. A clear recognition of her own competence would mean the loss of the weak, little-girl image to which she clung, in spite of its obvious inaccuracy. While some fear about the job seemed justified, her reluctance to relinquish the old image exaggerated the fears.

By contrast, a man, Charles, who was also very gifted, had the opportunity to take a higher-level job, and he was very pleased. In its administrative requirements and responsibilities it was similar to Mary's and was equally demanding. Just before he undertook the new job, he developed some fairly severe physical symptoms; characteristically he did not talk about them. His wife, Ruth, however, suspected that they were caused by his anxieties about facing the tasks ahead. Knowing him well, she did not mention the problem directly, but opened up the topic in the only way she felt able. She suggested that it might be a good idea to make some changes in their diet, hours, and general lifestyle. His initial reaction was one of anger; he disparaged her, sarcastically telling her to stop bothering him. Later he admitted to himself, and then to Ruth, that when he feels most uncertain of his abilities and most in need of help, he can react only with anger — especially if anyone seems to perceive his neediness.

Fortunately, Charles is trying hard to overcome the barriers that keep him from acknowledging these feelings. His wife's attempts opened up the possibility of dealing with them. He could not have initiated the process himself. He could not even respond to her initiation immediately, but this time, fairly soon after the fact he was able to catch himself in the act of denying it. Ruth easily might have remained rejected, hurt, and resentful, and the situation could have escalated into mutual anger and recrimination at the very time he was feeling most vulnerable, helpless, and needy.

It is important to note also that Ruth was *not* being rewarded for her strengths. Instead, she was made to suffer for them — by anger and rejection. This is a small example of how women's valuable qualities are not only not recognized but are punished instead. Even in this case, Ruth was not able to state her perceptions openly. She had to use "feminine wiles." Important qualities such as understanding of human vulnerabilities and offerings of help can thus be dysfunctional in relationships as they are presently structured and can make a woman feel she must be wrong.

In no society does the person — male or female — emerge full-grown. A necessary part of all experience is a recognition of one's weaknesses and limitations. That most valuable of human qualities — the ability to grow psychologically — is necessarily an ongoing process, involving repeated feelings of vulnerability all through life. As the example of Charles illustrates, men have been conditioned to fear and hate weakness, to try to get rid of it immediately and sometimes frantically. This attempt, I believe, represents an effort to distort human experience. It is necessary to "learn" in an emotional sense that these feelings are not shameful or abhorrent but ones from which the individual can move on — if the feelings are experienced for what they are. Only then can a person hope to find appropriate paths to new strengths. Along with new strength will come new areas of vulnerability, for there is no absolute invulnerability.

That women are better able than men to consciously admit to feelings of weakness or vulnerability may be obvious, but we have not recognized the importance of this ability. That women are truly much more able to tolerate these feelings — which life in general, and particularly in our society, generates in everybody — is a positive strength. Many adolescent boys and young men especially seem to be suffering acutely from the need to flee from these feelings *before* they experience them. In that sense, women, both superficially and deeply, are more closely in touch with basic life experiences — in touch with reality. By being in this closer connection with this central human condition, by having to defend less and deny less, women are in a position to understand weakness more readily and to work productively *with* it.

In short, in our society, while men are made to feel weak in many ways, women are made to feel weaker. But, because they "know" weakness, women can cease being the "carriers" of weakness and become the developers of a different understanding of it and of the appropriate paths out of it. Women, in undertaking their own journey, can illuminate the way for others.

Until now, women who are already strong in many ways still have had a hard time admitting it. Mary, the woman in the example, illustrates this problem. But even when weakness is real, women can go on to strength and ability once they can convince themselves that it is really all right to let go of their belief in the *rightness* of weakness. Only someone who understands women can understand how this psychic element operates, how widespread and influential the fear of *not* being weak can become, and how persistently it can hang on without being recognized for what it is. It is very difficult for men, with *their fears* of weakness, to see why women cling to it and to understand that it does not, and could not possibly, mean the same thing for women as it does for men.

There is a further social point here. The fact that these feelings are generally associated with being "womanly," — hence unmanly — serves to reinforce the humiliation suffered by the man who has such experiences. Women, in the meanwhile, provide all sorts of personal and social supports to help keep men going and to keep them and the total society from admitting that better arrangements are needed. That is, the whole man-woman interaction thus dilutes the push to confront and deal with our societal deficiencies. We all experience too much danger as we attempt to grow and make our way in the difficult and threatening circumstances in which we live. We all lose in the end, but the loss is kept obscure.

More can be understood of Charles' situation if we ask "what did he really want?" Like many people he wanted at least two things. He not only wanted them, he believed they were essential to his sense of self. He wanted, first of all, to sail through every situation feeling "like a man" — that is, strong, self-sufficient, and fully competent. He required of himself that he always feel this way. Anything less he experienced as a threat to his manliness. Such a requirement is unrealistic in the extreme, for we face repeated challenges in life; we are sure to feel doubts all along.

At the same time that Charles wanted to maintain this image of himself, he harbored the seemingly contradictory wish that his wife would somehow solve everything for him with such magic and dispatch that he would never be aware of his weakness at all. She should do this without being asked; it was essential that he never have to think or talk about his weakness. The fact that Ruth did not instantly accomplish this feat for him was a deep-seated cause of his anger at her.

Instead, she confronted him with an attempt to deal with the problem, and by doing so, she reminded him of his feelings of weakness and vulnerability. But even if she had done nothing, her very presence would have caused him to face the frustration of his wish for total caretaking and problem-solving. This sort of wish is prominent in many people and present to some extent in most. As long as women live under the major prescription that they please and serve men, they will be the objects of such desire. At the same time they will be unable to participate in the free-flowing mutual engagement and cooperation that can help them and others find ways of growing beyond this stage. The hope is that such wishes can be worked out and integrated on a more satisfactory level as one develops an increasing sense of one's own strengths and an increasing faith in other people. In this task, we need other people all through life, in adulthood no less than in childhood.

Initially, Ruth offered a step in this direction, a wholehearted attempt to help Charles and to struggle together with him. But this he could not accept. His refusal illustrates in a small way how women come to believe they are failures, even in the traditional wifely role. Since a major part of her sense of worth was based on her role as a wife, experiences of this kind could easily have undermined Ruth's self-confidence. She was well prepared to believe that her husband, as the man, was right and that she was wrong. To put this in a shorthand way, if the members of the dominant group — that is, men — claim that they do not have feelings of insecurity, subordinates (women) cannot challenge their claim. Furthermore, it is women's responsibility to supply the needs of the dominant group so that its members can continue to deny these feelings. The fact that such emotions are present in everyone and are intensified by the problems our society creates for all its people makes a difficult situation almost impossible.

With some couples, the mythology may seem to "work." Both partners know what is going on to some extent, and a balance is struck so that the arrangement is sufficiently satisfactory to sustain the status quo. The woman, considering the alternatives that faced her outside of marriage, was often willing to accept the situation. Such marriages, however, may create another kind of reaction in women.

In these situations, the women may be very wise in certain ways; but skilled as they are, they really know only half of the story, or perhaps less than half. The woman usually knows well her husband's areas of weakness, and she provides the needed supports. But even though such women may seem to function quite well in a home context, they increasingly develop the pervasive sense that, as keenly as they know the man's weaknesses, he must have an entirely unknown area of strength, some very important ability, that enables him to manage in "the real world." This element in him becomes increasingly foreign for the woman; it takes on the quality of an almost magical ability that men have and women do not.

Women sometimes come to look upon this manly quality as something they must *believe* in; it provides their major sense of support. Many women develop a great need to believe they have a strong man to whom they can turn for security and hope in the world. And, while it may seem improbable, this belief in the man's magical strength exists side by side with an intimate knowledge of the weaknesses to which she caters.

It is not simply that woman are obviously excluded from acquiring experience in the serious world of work, but that they actually come to believe that there is some special, inherent ability, some factor that escapes them and must inevitably escape them. The fact that women are themselves discouraged from serious testing of themselves fosters and deepens the need to believe that men have this special quality. Most women have a lifelong conditioning that induces them to believe this myth.

This very belief is one (but just one) of the expressions that psychiatrists and theorists have perceived as evidence of "penis envy." They may have been encouraged in their perception by the manner in which women talk of this "male quality" — as if it were some sort of magical and unattainable ability. Some men (perhaps those with more self-knowledge), knowing that they possess no extraordinary ability women do not share, have settled, for an explanation, on the most noticeable physical difference — the penis.

The truth would seem to be much simpler: that the only thing women lack is practice in the "real world"; this, plus the *opportunity* to practice and the lifelong belief that one has the *right* to do so. Such a simple statement, however, covers a great many complex psychological consequences.

New Paths Away from Weakness. The status quo is upset when one *admits* one's weakness publicly. The very fact of acknowledging feelings of weakness and vulnerability is new and original. The next step — the idea that women do not have to *remain* weak — is even more threatening. A hard question is joined when we ask what women can do about moving out of weakness. Here, women immediately run into opposition that can be very severe.

By acknowledging their weakness, women are undertaking, first of all, a vast act of exposure. As soon as women add, "I feel weak now, but I intend to move on from that," they are displaying a great strength, a form of strength that is particularly difficult for men. That is hard enough for men to take, but in addition, women are threatening to remove certain key props from men. It is particularly hard to endure someone's taking props away, but it is even harder if you have pretended all along that you did not need them in the first place.

Although real weaknesses are a problem for every human being, women's major difficulty lies more in admitting the strengths they already have and in allowing themselves to use their resources. Sometimes women already have the necessary resources or they clearly have a basis on which to build. In such instances, anxiety often arises. Indeed, the anxiety is greatly augmented by opposition both from our institutions and from people who are personally close. Women are confronted with obstacles on several levels: not only intrapsychic obstacles from their own pasts — which lead them to fear their strengths — but also obstacles in reality.

But when women begin to perceive forms of strength based on their own life experiences, rather than believing they should have the qualities they attribute to men, they often find new definitions of strength. A nice example of a strength translated into a social form is the patient-advocate system that has been developed by some women's health centers.

Almost everyone knows that confronting the doctor is a fearful prospect. In addition to fears about illness and its possible implications, a visit to a physician often touches off deeper fears of vulnerability, mutilation, and death. Women have recognized that it is very difficult to deal with these fears alone, especially when trying to cope with medical institutions as they are constituted today. In the patient-advocate system, an informed and experienced woman health worker goes along with the woman patient to the clinic or hospital and stays by her side, to speak up, to question, and to challenge. This example illustrates several of the elements to which I am pointing: it is easier for women to openly admit to their fears and, therefore, to identify their needs accurately. It is also easier for them to turn to others and ask for help. Clearly men need this help too. Once women have initiated this procedure perhaps men will adopt it, too — hopefully only as an interim measure until the field of medicine treats all people with greater sensitivity.

Vulnerability in Theory and Culture. As discussed so far, the feelings of weakness, vulnerability, and helplessness may sound commonplace. Our dealing with some of their more obvious implications has perhaps served to obscure their profound importance to the psychology community today. Indeed, current psychiatric thinking places them at the center of most problems. In the jargon of the field they have more impressive names, but the issues of how a person is made to feel vulnerable or helpless and what she/he then tries to do about it is probably the basic issue underlying most modern concerns in psychiatry. In its extreme form such vulnerability can be described as the threat of psychic annihilation, probably the most terrifying threat of all. People will do almost anything to avoid such threats.

There are differences in current psychiatric theory about both the origins of these threats and the form of the reactions they produce. Do they, for example, all originate primarily in separation anxiety in the infant, as John Bowlby postulates?[1] Or do they originate, as the Freudian and other instinct theories propose, because one's instinctual impulses clash with the "real world," leading one to feel weak and vulnerable (in addition to other things)? Whether any current or past theories explain the origins of these feelings adequately, all of them grew out of a culture that has made one sex the embodiment of weakness and the other the embodiment of strength. The new feature is that women are now in a position to open up a new and potentially radically different perspective on this topic.

Psychoanalytic theories, stated simply, hold that one attempts to develop ways to deal with these feelings, mental mechanisms that enable a person to overcome feelings of vulnerability and helplessness. Accordingly, people construct an inner scheme of things by which they believe they will gain satisfaction and safety. The scheme can become very complex and quite rigid. People often are convinced that they need to relate to the world and people in it in a certain fixed manner, and they may react forcefully if they cannot bring about the desired situation or relationship.

One way of describing all psychological problems might be to say that people believe they can be safe and satisfied only if they complete and can force others to complete a certain picture of what they need. If they cannot accomplish this, they feel weak and vulnerable. These feelings are so dreadful that people then push even harder to make their particular schemes come about.

These dreaded feelings — inherent in the human condition — have been associated with women and babies. Both those who *experience* them and those who *respond* to them are covered with derision. Males are "allowed" to have them for only a short period in infancy; after that, they are expected to be virtually done with them for life. Our psychological theories reflect this situation; indeed our very basic model of the human mind is one in which emotional weaknesses are said to be crucially dealt with and almost rigidly fixed in the early years of infancy. This model may have something to do with male culture's attempts to rid men of these experiences.

The second great theme revolves around the relation of other people to these threats. In modern living, the major threats come not from the physical world but from other people; it is people who make us feel vulnerable, from early childhood and on throughout life. If one could turn readily to other people in seeking to deal with these feelings, if one could do this repeatedly with faith and ease, there would be many more chances of productively dealing with life.

Emotions

Emotionality, as part and parcel of every state of being, is even more basic than feelings of vulnerability and weakness. In our dominant tradition, however, it has not been seen as an aid to understanding and action, but rather as an impediment, even an evil. We have a long tradition of trying to dispense with, or at least to control or neutralize, emotionality, rather than valuing, embracing, and cultivating its contributing strengths. At this time most women do have a much greater sense of the emotional components of all human activity than most men. This is, in part, a result of their training as subordinates; for anyone in a subordinate position must learn to be attuned to the vicissitudes of mood, pleasure, and displeasure of the dominant group. Black writers have made this point very clearly. Subordinate groups can use these developed abilities as one of the few weapons available in the struggle with the dominants, and women have often done so. "Womanly intuition" and "womanly wiles" are examples. But, however attained, these qualities bespeak a basic ability that is very valuable. It can hardly be denied that emotions are essential aspects of human life.

Men are encouraged from early life to be active and rational; women are trained to be involved with emotions and with the feelings occurring in the course of all activity. Out of this, women have gained the insight that events are important and satisfying only if they occur within the context of emotional relatedness. They are more likely than men to believe that, ideally, all activity should lead to an increased emotional connection with others. However, psychological and social difficulties have come from the distortions taught to women. Indeed, women have been led to believe that if they act and think effectively they will jeopardize their chances for satisfying emotional experience. Such precepts have led to terrible twists, so that women are made to feel that their strongest assets are really liabilities.

Another aspect is important. Women have been so encouraged to concentrate on the emotions and reactions of others that they have been diverted from examining and expressing their own emotions. While this is very understandable, given the past situation, women have not yet fully applied this highly developed faculty to exploring and knowing *themselves.*

Many women are currently in the process of doing just this in a new way. Some of the places to which their explorations have led will be explored further in later chapters. But to understand thoroughly the situation that still exists for most women, we may return to Ruth. Ruth's experience offers a brief illustration of how strength can be made to seem a weakness. Because of her well-developed ability to attend to emotions, Ruth was more able to grasp the totality of Charles' situation. But the opportunity to let her understanding unfold and to act on it to find a solution was obstructed by her husband's dictum. Ruth retreated, feeling inadequate, a failure, and certain that she must be wrong about the whole thing.

Participating in the Development of Others

There is no question that the dominant society has said, men will do the important work; women will tend to the "lesser task" of helping other human beings to develop. At the outset this dichotomy means that our major societal institutions are *not* founded on the tenet of helping others to develop. All people need help in development at all stages, but it is made to appear as if only children do. This casts both women and children under a pall, with many psychological consequences for children of both sexes. The person most intimately involved in their development is seen as a lesser figure performing a lesser task, even though she is of pre-eminent importance to them. Further, women have had to do this major work without the supports that a culture would give to a task it valued. But the fact is women have done it nonetheless.

Despite all the handicaps, women have a much greater sense of the pleasures of close connection with physical, emotional, and mental growth than men. Growth is one of the — perhaps the — most important, most exciting qualities of being human. Tragically, in our society, women are prevented from fully enjoying these pleasures themselves by being made to feel that fostering them in others is the only valid role for all women and by the loneliness, drudgery, and isolated, noncooperative household setting in which they work.

Participation in others' growth is one of the major satisfactions in psychotherapy. To be part of the experience of another person's struggle to break through to a new and satisfying way of seeing, feeling, or acting is extremely gratifying. Good therapists know that it is the client's own effort, but they also know that they can play an important facilitating part.

From this participation, a therapist can derive great pleasure. But this is the same sort of basic activity that women are performing every day.

Women have now stated that helping in the growth of others without the equal opportunity and right to growth for themselves is a form of oppression. In fact, in our unequal situation, the valuable part of women's participation in others' development is in constant danger of degenerating into the provision of mere ego-support — what Jessie Bernard has described as the "stroking" function.[2] Here again, inequality distorts and negates a valuable ability. Ruth is an example of a woman trying to assist in growth but being pushed toward mere "stroking." In later chapters, we will discuss even more serious ways in which this valuable quality is distorted.

Cooperation

Another important aspect of women's psychology is their greater recognition of the essential cooperative nature of human existence. Despite the competitive aspects of any society, there must be a bedrock modicum of cooperativeness for society to exist at all. (I define cooperative as behavior that aids and enhances the development of other human beings while advancing one's own.) It is certainly clear that we have not reached a very high level of cooperative living. To the extent that it exists, women have assumed the greater responsibility for providing it. Although they may not label it in large letters, women in families are constantly trying to work out some sort of cooperative system that attends to each person's needs. Their task is greatly impeded by the unequal premise on which our families are based, but it has been women who have *practiced* trying.

Take the example of Mary, who was worried about a new, demanding job. If she took the job, she would need a new level of cooperation from her husband, Joe. If he were able to provide it, he would seem a most unusual man. Mary had been giving *him* and the children that kind of cooperative support for years.

Joe may seem to have come out of nowhere at this time. His

absence from the discussion until now makes an interesting point. For Joe is, in fact, a "nice guy." He and Mary love and respect each other. "He doesn't stop me from working," says Mary. "He helps me out in a pinch and is often kind and understanding." He does not feel, however, that working out ways to provide the maximum development of everyone in the family is his major responsibility. That is Mary's job.

Women's cooperative tendency, even in the midst of severe psychological problems, was evident in the situation of another couple. Jim was a person with severe problems; he had become addicted to drugs and was progressively deteriorating. His wife, Helen, too, had deep-seated difficulties. After several years spent attacking and diminishing each other, Jim felt he could no longer face anything and he disappeared. In part, he left because he was deeply ashamed of himself and his repeated failure in practically all areas of life. Although trained as a lawyer, he felt by that time that he had nothing left. Helen, on the other hand, though equally ashamed and destroyed, did not leave, much as she, too, may have wished to do so. Although she certainly felt unable to offer anything to anybody, she remained to take care of her three children. As deprived and empty as she herself felt, she hung on in a desperate effort to do whatever she could for them. For a long initial period, she felt it was only her sense of the children's needs that kept her barely moving through the days and surviving through the nights. Eventually, she built many more resources and now says, "I never knew I could be the person I feel today."

Leaving out the long intervening struggle, the point to be made here is that Helen struggled to make something work even though "only the children seemed to have any real reason to live." She still felt the need to engage in some kind of cooperative functioning and a *desire* to do it, even though she could barely manage. The same motivation was not there in any meaningful way for Jim. I have seen examples of this with many other couples.

While men do enter into some forms of concerted endeavor, the prevailing values in the settings in which most men spend their lives make it extremely difficult to sustain it. Moreover, in the family setting, men very early in life acquire the sense that they are members of a superior group. Things are supposed to be done for them by those lesser people who work at trying to do so. From then on, cooperativeness may appear to men as if it were somehow detracting from themselves. To cooperate, to share, means somehow to lose something, or at best, altruistically, to give something away. All this is greatly augmented by men's notions that they must be independent, go it alone, win.

To women, who do not have the same experience, cooperativeness does not have the same quality of loss. In the first place, most women have not been imbued with a spurious sense of advantage over a group of other people.

By saying that women are more practiced in cooperation and that women are at present more able to seek out and enjoy situations that require that quality, I do not mean that women have any greater inherent saintliness, but rather, that life so far has led women to this position. Today, as women try to move on, they are finding not only more necessity but also more desire to consciously struggle for even more cooperation. We all know that women have many competitive aspects, too. Both tendencies exist in each sex but in different proportions. In the past, many women were concerned with competing with each other for men, for obvious reasons. Many women are now trying to turn away from this sort of competition with other women, shifting the balance even further toward cooperativeness.

Creativity

Creativity, taken together with cooperativeness, leads to an overall proposition — and a return to the earlier discussion about psychoanalysis. I have been underlining that psychoanalysis has been pointing out aspects of absolute human necessity; I have said also that these areas of life — such as sexuality and emotional connectedness — are the very realms generally relegated to woman. I should now like to propose that there is yet a third area of absolute human necessity that psychoanalysis has not yet "unearthed" or delineated even as imperfectly as it has defined the issue of sexuality or the nature of basic emotional connections. Not surprisingly, this area has also been denied explicit recognition by the dominant culture. I refer to the absolute necessity of, and the absolute existence in human beings of, the potential for both cooperation and creativity. It is clear that the thwarting of these necessities, the blocking of these needs, produces as many, or more, problems than anything so far delineated in psychodynamics. For emphasis, I will call this consideration the third stage of psychoanalysis.

I am not referring in this context to the creativity in artistic productions by the gifted few but to the intense personal creating that we each must do all through life. *Everyone* repeatedly has to break through to a new vision if she/he is to keep living. This very personal kind of creativity, this making of new visions, this continuous struggle, does not usually go on in open and well-articulated ways. But it goes on. Today, we can see this universal process most clearly in women. Women are the people struggling to create for themselves a new concept of personhood; they are attempting to restructure the central tenets of their lives. This effort extends to the deepest inner reaches.

But even in the past, it was women who had to innovate their inner psychological structures in order to survive at all within the dominant culture. Society arranged for, and by, men institutes key social-psychological guidelines and values that are not really applicable to women. (The well-known Broverman study has provided documentation on this point.[3]) Women have grown up knowing the goals most valued for individual development were not to be *their* goals. On the other hand, women do grow and develop. They have constructed an inner person who is different from the person most valued in this society.

Women have always had to come up with a basis for worthiness that is different from that which the dominant culture bestows. They have effected enough of a creative internal transformation of values to allow themselves to believe that caring for people and participating in others' development is enhancing to self-esteem. In this sense, even women who live by all of the old stereotypes are in advance of the values of this society. This does not mean they are therefore recognized and rewarded for their value system. Quite pointedly, they are not; they are made to feel that they are of little worth — "I am only a housewife and mother."

Some women have managed to create other roles for themselves to contribute to their sense of self-esteem. But a woman who has done so has violated a dominant system of values that says she is not worthy; indeed, it implies that there must be something wrong with her for even wanting alternatives. However, any woman who has gone beyond the assigned tasks has already created an inner conception by which she is guided, which sustains her, however imperfectly. Exactly what internal conception each woman creates is often difficult to tease out explicitly. In most cases, such conceptions are not fully stated and clarified in words.

Today, women are struggling to go on from this point to create a new kind of person in a much bolder, more thoroughgoing, and conscious way. In recent years it has become apparent that women must create new conceptions of what it means to be a person if they are to change the day-to-day workings of their lives. When women seriously resist the old internal and external proscriptions and demands they *have* to find new conceptions to live by. They are also the people most stimulated to be imaginative and adventurous.

As women change, they will create severe challenges. To suggest just one, when more women refuse, thoroughly and totally, to allow themselves to be used as objects, either in the grossest commercial form or in the most intimate personal encounter whom will society then use as objects? If there is no one to use, what kinds of revolutionary personal transformations will the dominant group have to make for itself? Will this not end in liberating some of the creative potential in men?

These are some of the concerns with which women have had to grapple in the past, often in lonely, isolated, and frightening ways. They are now beginning to deal with them in cooperative ways with large numbers of other women. The cooperativeness and creativity that I think exists in all people, that has been essential to all human life, is now being raised to a more conscious level and made explicit.

Women in the past have been led to believe that they had no special contribution to make. If women tried to move beyond the limited assigned area, they felt that they must somehow rush to catch up to, or to catch on to, the dominant group's interests and concerns. It is clear today that there are vast areas in which our dominant society is failing. As women recognize their strengths and as they raise their very own concerns, they can, not only progress toward a new synthesis, but simultaneously clarify and make much more obvious the issues central to all human beings.

What about men in all this? Here I would like to return to some of Freud's own last words on the subject, which we can now see in a different light.[4] Freud said that the basic thing that men struggled against is identification with the female, which, a psychoanalyst would immediately have to say, also implies the desire for that identification. I would like to suggest that men struggle not against identification with the female *per se* in a concrete sense, but that men do indeed struggle to reclaim the very parts of their own experience that they have delegated to women. Men, I think, would enjoy great comfort and growth in being able more fully to integrate and reintegrate these parts of themselves. They desire to recapture without shame the experience of their various vicissitudes and struggles, which represent the inevitable problems of growing up and of living with one's total being in our imperfect society; they desire to recapture those parts of themselves which have dreaded and frightening properties for men, but which have been made much more frightening because they have been labeled "female."

As women refuse to become the carriers of some of the central unsolved problems of male-led society, and as women move on to become the proponents of some of the best parts of human potential, we will, I think, create a climate in which men will face the challenge of grappling with their own issues in their own way. Men will be faced with having to deal with their bodily, their sexual, their childish experiences, their feelings of weakness, vulnerability, helplessness, and the other similar unsolved areas. But men can also go on to enlarge their emotional experience and more fully discover their real potential for cooperativeness and creativity. As these areas are no longer "filled in" by women and devalued by a male-led society, men will be forced to confront the ways in which their social forms do not adequately deal with these necessities. They will have to go about finding their own newer and better ways.

It may be useful to summarize the foregoing. I believe that women can value their psychological qualities in a new way as they recognize the origins and functions of these qualities. Throughout this book, I emphasize the two sides of these strengths. Eventually, we can hope to place them within a fuller theory of women's development. But even now, we can recognize that women's psychological strengths are not perceived as such by the dominant group.

I do not imply that women should go back into some supportive role. It is the reverse. Women can go on to greatly enlarge their scope and activity, building on a base that is already valuable.

It is possible that this may sound as if I am claiming that women are better because they have suffered more — or that women are more virtuous. I am not addressing this issue. What I *do* see is that our dominant society is a very imperfect one. It is a low-level, primitive organization built on an exceedingly restricted conception of the total human potential. It holds up narrow and ultimately destructive goals for the dominant group and attempts to deny vast areas of life. The falsity and the full impact of this limited conception has been obscured. Significantly, women have now elucidated one large and central part of this impact — precisely because women are the people who receive this impact.

Some of the areas of life denied by the dominant group are relegated and projected onto all subordinate groups, not solely women. This partakes of the familiar scapegoat process. But other parts of human experience are so necessary that they cannot be projected very far away. One must *have* them nearby, even if one can still deny *owning* them. These are the special areas delegated to women. Based on their intimate experiences with them, women feel the problems in these areas most acutely, but they are even further diminished if they mention the unmentionable, expose certain key problems. This proscription has kept women from seeing that they have different desires and ways of living than those recognized and rewarded by the dominant culture. In this, women can indeed be seen to be "ahead" of psychological theory and practice — and of the culture that gave rise to present theory.

chapter five

doing good and feeling bad

The overall attempt of this book is to look toward a more accurate understanding of women's psychology as it arises out of women's life experience rather than as it has been perceived by those who do not have that experience. In doing so, we have suggested in the last chapter a possible third stage of psychoanalysis or of psychodynamic understanding — one in which cooperation and creativity assume their full and rightful place. We have postulated that this third stage may become explicit through women's effort to act on their situation — the basic proposition being that the prior two stages are linked to women's situation too but have not been recognized as such.

It is important, however, to step back and fill in — first, to suggest briefly a few more of the valuable characteristics that women develop. While in some ways these cut across all of the psychoanalytic stages, as it were, they are particularly important in looking toward the third stage, that is, toward an advance in psychological understanding.

Second, it is important to describe the complexities involved in the process by which these strengths have been made to seem like weaknesses, and how this has affected and still affects women. The latter part of this chapter, at least briefly, will discuss feminine failure and "feminine evil."

49

Giving

In psychotherapy, women often spend a great deal more time talking about giving than men do. Women constantly confront themselves with questions about giving. Am I giving enough? Can I give enough? Why don't I give enough? They frequently have deep fears about what this must mean about them. They are upset if they feel they are not givers. They wonder what would happen if they were to stop giving, to even consider not giving? The idea is frightening and the consequences too dire to consider. Outside of a clinical setting, most women do not even dare to suggest openly such a possibility.

By contrast, the question of whether he is a giver or giving enough does not enter into a man's self-image. Few men feel that giving is a primary issue in their struggles for identity. They are concerned much more about "doing." Am I a doer? Do I measure up to the proper image of someone who does? While job performance may result in giving to the family financially, this kind of giving has a different connotation. It is not an integral part of the self-image for which a man strives. In fact, to be seen as too much of a giver is something of a detraction, implying that one is a little too soft, a bit of a patsy.

Here, as in the area of weakness and vulnerability, I believe that many men clearly long to give of themselves. Further, I know a number of adolescent boys yearning to give to others, but they cannot find a way to do so that will contribute to their sense of identity. For men, giving is clearly an added luxury that is allowed only *after* they have fulfilled the primary requirements of manhood.

This asymmetrical distribution of the human possibilities of giving leads to many complications. An important example occurs in the area of sex. Even though it may not be admitted in these days of the so-called sexual revolution, many young women still feel deeply they are giving something to the man by having sexual relations with him. One young woman I have talked with, Nancy — whose sexual style may have seemed very casual — had such feelings. By contrast, her male partners felt either that they had succeeded in "doing" something or that they had "taken" something from her.

For young women like Nancy, this long-held interpretation of sexuality as giving had several complicating sides. Nancy's focus on that one aspect was one of many factors that served to obscure full recognition of, and forthright dealing with, her own sexual desires. There is, as we know, a long historical development of that attitude, and the problems it bred are still very much with us. The point is that most women still cannot engage in sexual relations without the feeling that they are "primarily" giving to the other person. But isn't this true? In fact, in sexual relations *each* person does give to the other in a very basic sense. It could not be otherwise. This is an obvious truth that male thinking about sex has gone a long way to obscure.

It is interesting to note that the new forms of therapy for sexual problems focus simultaneously on giving *and* on taking responsibility for one's own pleasure. That is, each person not only has to admit to her/his role as a giver, but also must accept her/his role as a receiver of pleasure. Current authorities attribute many male sexual difficulties to a misguided preoccupation with performance rather than pleasure. This preoccupation has often diverted men from developing both the ability to allow the flow of pleasure and the ability to perceive that the giving of pleasure is an essential part of sexual satisfaction. Unfortunately, many women, too, have recently become caught up in the male view of sex as performance.

There are many other realms in which the assignment to women of the role of giver leads to problems. As wives, mothers, daughters, lovers, or workers, women often feel that other people are demanding too much of them; and they resent it. Frequently they cannot even allow themselves to admit that they resent these excess pressures. They have come to believe that they should *want* to respond at all times and in all ways. Consequently, they cannot let themselves openly call a halt to the demands or even take small steps to limit them. The hesitation to do this, to resist control of their own lives in even ordinary ways, can result in many psychological complications or even somatic symptoms. Such symptoms are often indirect ways of saying, among other things, "I can't give anymore, but I don't feel allowed to stop."

One woman, Florence, experienced recurrent episodes of abdominal and pelvic pain, for which there was no physical cause. After long exploration, she discovered that these attacks occurred when her children put excessive demands on her. By contrast, her husband was not, in any case, the usual recipient of their demands. On the occasions when the demands were directed to him, he either did not perceive them or, when he felt like it, said "No." Florence's situation was not a simple one. It was embedded in a background in which her mother had seemed to her to be endlessly giving. "My mother never said 'No.'" This early experience was crucial to Florence's notion of what it meant to be a woman.

Clearly, women need to allow themselves to take, openly, as well as give. They are now in a unique position to integrate taking and giving in a new and more mutual way. Our culture thus far has prevented men from integrating giving as a major feature of their self-image. But as women seek this new integration they will be working against complicated opposition. (They will even be called selfish!)

It is important to understand that, in the traditional relationship, men are giving in a circumscribed way to *lesser* beings — women and children. A man can seldom give fully to his "equals" — that is, other men — directly. If he does, he may be characterized as a less important creature, for to be important — and even to be safe — he must strive for power over his "equals," other men. Thus, both sexes have been deprived of the possibility of developing as people who have the experience of giving to equals and realizing that such mutual kinds of giving are possible and can enhance the development of all.

Activity – Passivity

There is the old shibboleth that men are active and women are passive. Added to it is modern psychology's dictum that, in order not to diminish men's masculinity, women *should* be passive. All of this has created a great deal of confusion and trouble.

Helen, whose husband was the drug-addicted lawyer mentioned in the last chapter, offers one example of the manner in which women's activity is overlooked, even by women themselves. Helen did not think of herself as particularly intelligent; she believed that there was nothing she could really do well, although she had competently run a middle-class household and entertained lavishly, to advance her husband's career prior to the family's deterioration. She also took care of the children and arranged for extra educational and developmental activities that the social-climbing lawyer wanted for them — music and dancing lessons, athletics, tutoring, and the like. In addition, she acted as her husband's receptionist and secretary. As Jim became more addicted and unable to function, she took care of a large part of his legal work for him. For months she untangled the consequences of missed appointments and other lapses and handled numerous clients' affairs as she kept up a front for him. Despite all this, Helen reiterated that there was nothing she knew how to do. In one sense, she meant that she had no formal credentials readily usable in the economic market; but she also still suffered deeply from the inner conviction that she "really couldn't do anything."

In society's terms, Helen was not entirely wrong, for, in a general way, male society recognizes as activity only what men do. And, if women somehow manage to do what men do, they are strongly, even violently, opposed. We can still witness genuine resistance amongst male physicists to the presence of a woman physicist. Despite recent changes this kind of reaction may prevent women from openly letting men know that they can do what men can do.

Most so-called women's work is not recognized as real activity. One reason for this attitude may be that such work is usually associated with helping others' development, rather than with self-enhancement. This is seen as *not doing anything*. Here again, we see how one's perceptions influence one's definition of what is happening and one's ability to call it by a name that elucidates the truth about what is occurring. Ruth, for example, who was trying to help her husband with his job-related symptoms, may have been seen as "doing nothing."

There is no question that women are performing activity all of the time; but it is also true that most of this activity has not been done in direct and open pursuit of their own goals — therefore it is not activity in the male definition of it. Further, when they do pursue their self-interests, women have difficulty in allowing this kind of activity to be a basis for a sense of their self-worth. Women's sense of worth is not supposed to come from this quarter. On the contrary, any activity oriented toward a personal goal can easily become fraught with conflict and can contribute to *diminishing* a woman's self-image. (This activity is not what a woman is supposed to use to build a sense of worthiness!) Indeed, this is a central way in which women have been seriously deprived: a woman cannot use her own life activity to build an image of herself based on an authentic reflection of what she actually is and does.

On the other hand, women have traditionally built a sense of self-worth on activities that they can manage to define as taking care of and giving to others. (If they can convince themselves that they are doing a job that can be defined in this way, they can accomplish tremendous things. This dynamic will be discussed more fully in the next chapter.) This situation is complex because even out of this traditional setting a valuable tendency arises. Women, more easily than men, can believe that any activity is more satisfying when it takes place in the context of relationships to other human beings — and even more so when it leads to the enhancement of others. Women *know* this experience in a way that men do not.

There is much more to be elucidated about the quality of women's activity. For example, many of the activities that women do best are incorrectly defined as if they were merely passive. In fact, the word "passivity" is currently used to cover a great variety of behaviors and experiences that are really quite different. Listening to another, taking in, receiving, or accepting from another, are often seen as passive. However, they all generate a response, for one never merely passively receives; one also reacts. The reaction can take many forms. It is true that men feel more pressured to cut short their receptiveness and to rush to put forward their own reactions. Often they clearly betray the fact that they have not received or heard much of what the other was communicating. Women, on the other hand, have often heard much more than was overtly stated and have gone through a more complex processing of information. Part of this processing, especially the part men are not permitted to observe, includes the knowledge that one had better not react directly and honestly to what has been said or done. This avoidance of direct expression has often been misinterpreted as evidence of inherent passivity.

Change

The very essence of all life is growth, which means change. The one great additional feature that characterizes human growth is psychological change. People who are most attuned to psychological growth are those most closely in touch with it, those who are literally forced to keep changing if they are to continue to respond to the altering demands of those under their care. For an infant and then a child to grow there must be someone who can respond to the child. As the child grows, one's responses must change accordingly. What sufficed today will not suffice tomorrow. The child has come to a different place, and the caretaker must move to another place too. If you are the caretaker you keep trying to do so.

Thus, in a very immediate and day-to-day way women *live* change. It is amazing, in view of this, that women have been portrayed as the traditionalists, the sex that upholds the past while men march on to "progress." Here is perhaps one of the major places we have fallen into a terrible twisting of reality, for if anything women are *closer* to change, real change. They have always been closest to direct involvement in the most important growth of all.[1]

For human beings it is absolutely true that life is not only biological, it is also psychological and intellectual. The mind is constantly pushing toward growth. It cannot stand still, nor can it really go backward to some earlier level of organization. Although we all know this, we have not really taken it into account.

What is it then that does not change, or resists change? It is quite clear that there is an inherent tendency for societies to maintain themselves and for those in positions of prestige and power to believe in and seek to maintain fixity. This is a truism. The leadership of a society has never been voluntarily relinquished. Even leaders of the utmost honesty cannot usually conceive that it would be right to do so.

Men, in our society and in most others, are encouraged from early in life to incorporate and to aim toward living up to the highest values of their society. They are much more thoroughly and internally formed by these precepts than are women, much more in tune with the status quo.

Change requires learning. But the specific processes involved in women's learning are submerged and go unrecognized because the dominant culture describes learning only in accordance with its own interests and understanding. In our culture, the respected explanations are created in the domains of science, which are quite removed from the direct life of growth and change. The following example of this difference was suggested by Anita Mishler, an astute educator.[2] Most learning, as studied and therefore as understood by our scientists, is only one general sort of learning. One learns how to do something or learns how something operates and then goes on to apply it *exactly* as one has learned it, or one generalizes from it to other situations. Raising children is an example of a totally different kind of learning. What one learned yesterday is not good enough and does not apply today. One cannot hope to use it exactly, nor even by analogy, because the situation has already changed. Thus, what women are doing in an everyday-kind-of way involves a different kind of learning. (It is important to note that this more complex learning occurs also in women who do not have children. Girls develop it through childhood and continue the process as they grow up.)

Awareness of this idea opens up the prospect of a new way of studying learning. Such a study may come about when we attend to what goes on in women's lives that is different from what goes on in men's. It points to the reality that change and growth are intimate parts of women's lives in a way in which they are not for men. Most important of all, it may bring about a concept of learning for change rather than for fixity, a concept that is crucial for societies but has not yet been grasped.

Some societies, particularly ours, attempt to divert the need for change by entertainment, and a rapid succession of fads. All of these "circuses" may convey the illusion of change, but in fact they accomplish the opposite. They do not meet the need for growth and enlargement of the mind. Instead, they often confuse us so much that we overlook the terrible frustration of this true need. They thwart rather than fulfill it.

Today, as women turn to the issue of their own development and enlargement, they are confronting society with *real* change, change in the very basis of everyone's existence and the way each person defines her or his self. Women now face the task of putting their vast unrecognized experience with change into a new and broader level of operation. Women are the people who have the need and motivation to make major changes in their way of living. As they initiate the changes required to meet their own needs they will create the stimulus for a thoroughgoing overhaul of the entire society.

Feminine Evil and Women's Sense of Failure

So far, we have barely listed some of the womanly qualities that should be considered strengths. Before attempting to integrate these into a more ordered picture, it is important to pursue further the reasons that these qualities, which may seem quite obvious, can become so confused and obscure. In short, it is necessary to ask the question: if they are all so good, why do women feel so bad?

As we have suggested, women are constantly confronting men with man's unsolved problems or challenging them with men's own unrealized potential. If women step beyond the bounds of the realms assigned to them, they cannot help but confront and challenge men. But even in their traditional roles, women, by *their very existence,* confront and challenge men because they have been made *the embodiment of the dominant culture's unsolved problems.* Further, if women act at all honestly and authentically out of their own experience in the *only* realms assigned to them, they will still discomfort men.

This confrontation and challenge could even now be a constant learning, growing encounter for both. But, as the situation has been structured so far, the possibility is most difficult to realize. Since women have had to live by trying to please men, they have been conditioned to prevent men from feeling even uncomfortable. Moreover, when women suspect that they have caused men to feel unhappy or angry, they have a strong tendency to assume that they themselves are wrong.

Producing discomfort or displeasure is one thing if a person has the conviction that she/he has a valid reason for doing so, or if she/he can recognize a right to do so. Even more fundamentally, if one has some way of conceptualizing and understanding events, even if one is not always absolutely certain, one may be psychologically prepared to risk causing discomfort. When, however, we can think only in terms given by the dominant culture, and when that culture not only does not attend to our own experiences but specifically denies and devalues them, we are left with no way of conceptualizing our lives. Under these circumstances, a woman is often left with a global, undefined sense that she must be wrong. Ruth, for instance, whose husband was starting a new job, was in that position.

All these mechanisms, and more, obscure the real situation of inequality which afflicts women. The "more" follows from the fact that no person really experiences such effacement and denial of her or his own experience without simultaneously reacting to it. One is hurt, or, even worse, one feels the threat of annihilation of one's whole being. One also becomes angry but has nowhere to go with this anger, no way to understand it.

The anger adds further to the sense of being wrong. Now, one builds up a store of angry negative emotions, feeling not only wrong, but — much more frightening — *bad* and *evil*.

Male culture has built an amazingly large mythology around the idea of feminine evil — Eve, Pandora's box, and the like. All this mythology seems clearly to be linked to *men's* unsolved problems, the things *they* fear they will find if they open Pandora's box. Women, meanwhile, have been prepared to stand ready and willing to accept all that evil. Women are thus caught with no real power in a situation militating toward failure. They not only feel like failures but come to believe that failure further confirms their evilness. (In our society, especially, we tend to incorporate the notion that success confirms goodness.)

Women, themselves, are simultaneously likely to feel most keenly the direct effects of our societies' deepest problems. To touch on one large area, our culture tends to "objectify" people, that is, to treat most people as if they were things; it treats women almost totally in this way. To be considered as an object can lead to the deep inner sense that there must be something wrong and bad about oneself. Workers on an assembly line have felt this dehumanization, and students have protested about it in past decades. Women feel it not only because it is pervasive in the dominant society but also because it is carried into their most intimate relationships. To be treated like an object is to be threatened with psychic annihilation. It is a truly dreadful experience. Several writers have popularized the role it plays in severe psychological troubles (e.g., R. D. Laing), but most have not highlighted the point that this factor is intrinsic to the most central relationship — the crucible of all relationships — the woman-man relationship. I emphasize it here because of the part it can contribute to a woman's belief that there must be something terribly bad and evil about her. It must be true, since others, the important and worthy others, seem to think she deserves to be treated as an object. Objectification adds a deep and thoroughgoing reason for women's readiness to accept the evil assigned to them.

One dimension of objectification, the experience of being

made a sex object, is a particularly destructive one. Many women writers have described their depths of humiliation in this situation and also the fact that they have been made to feel evil and wrong in the end. Only one facet will be emphasized here: when one is an object, not a subject, all of one's own physical and sexual impulses and interests are presumed not to exist independently. They are to be brought into existence only by and for others — controlled, defined, and used. Any stirrings of physicality and sexuality in herself would only confirm for a girl or woman her evil state. This is one of the most striking and tragic examples of how inequality enlists some of a woman's own marvelous qualities in the service of her enslavement and degradation.[3] (And then a term like inherent masochism is coined!)[4]

chapter six

serving others' needs — doing for others

In our culture "serving others" is for losers, it is low-level stuff. Yet serving others is a basic principle around which women's lives are organized; it is far from such for men. In fact, there are psychoanalytic data to suggest that men's lives are psychologically organized *against* such a principle, that there is a potent dynamic at work forcing men *away* from such a goal.[1]

The *Integrating Element*

Obviously people have to serve each other's needs, since human beings have needs. Who will serve them if not other people?

The organization of one's life around serving others is such a central factor for women that most of the topics mentioned bear a close relation to this general theme. Indeed, it can be seen as an overriding one. Eventually we may be able to state it as a more precise and dynamic formulation. For the present it is of extreme importance to stress that women have been led to feel that they can integrate and use all their attributes if they use them for others, but not for themselves. They have developed the sense that their lives should be guided by the constant need to attune themselves to the wishes, desires, and needs of others. The others are the important ones and the guides to action.

While men are also influenced by the judgments of other people and are affected by them in a variety of ways, there is a major difference. It is that men are judged, and they judge themselves, in terms of how well they themselves measure up to the demands of their culture. It is not so for women.

This difference is closely related to the psychoanalytic theory of ego development. Indeed, the ego, the "I" of psychoanalysis, may not be at all appropriate when talking about women. Women have different organizing principles around which their psyches are structured. One of these principles is that they exist to serve other people's needs. The fundamental nature of the difference between this organizing principle and the traditional delineation of the ego will be noted here and returned to later.

As with other topics we have discussed, women's experience of serving others has two sides; and each side, in turn, has its complexities. Women are taught that their main goal in life is to serve others — first men, and later, children. This prescription leads to enormous problems, for it is supposed to be carried out as if women did not have needs of their own, as if one could serve others without simultaneously attending to one's own interests and desires. Carried to its "perfection," it produces the martyr syndrome or the smothering wife and mother. But there is also, in this, a path for more advanced development. Women do have a much greater and more refined ability to encompass others' needs and to do this with ease. By this I mean that women are better geared than men to first recognize others' needs and then to believe strongly that others' needs can be served — that they can respond to others' needs without feeling this as a detraction from their sense of identity. The trouble comes only when women are *forced* to serve others' needs or when they are expected to do so because it is the "only thing women are good for."

Moreover, until recently, few opportunities for simultaneous self-development and service to others have existed; there were virtually no social forms in which this combination could be put into operation. If such forms were available, I believe that women could enter into them without the kind of conflict that confronts men. The problem is that they do not exist. For men the prospect of combining self-development with service to others seems an impossibly complex proposition. For women this complexity is not so great. The possibility is much easier to contemplate than the thinking of the dominant group would allow.

It was this factor that affected Mary, the woman discussed in Chapter Four, who worried about accepting a more demanding job. She saw herself as someone who wanted to serve the needs of others and who attained satisfaction in doing so. This ability was one of the sources of her fine performance at her work, as well as one component of her inner sense of worth. The new job would make it more difficult to continue to exercise this strength, both in the work itself and in her close personal relationships. This limitation augmented her conflict. If the job scheduling had been rearranged so as to allow her the room to continue serving her family in her usual way, she would have experienced much less conflict. One can *see* ways to easily rearrange job and home schedules for both women and men. To actually *do* so will require a major change in our institutions and work places. By contrast, such considerations did not enter into Charles' estimates about his new job. Instead, his wife was performing this kind of service for *him*, with her perceptive attempts to relieve his symptoms.

To say that women believe they *must* serve others may seem a commonplace observation. In fact, within social arrangements as they have been, the assignment of this role has cut very deep and created a number of psychological complexities. Unfortunately, it is such a common and ordinary observation in the psychological community that many people miss its overwhelming importance as a factor in creating problems for women. This happens when clinicians accept it as "just part of the usual backdrop," not realizing that many women truly cannot *tolerate or allow themselves* to feel that their life activities are for themselves. Such a situation, in itself, runs counter to most modern assumptions about the origins of psychological "health" — which posit an enlightened self-interest — but this obvious contradiction is not usually noticed. In fact, the situation is even more complex than this.

At the outset, one reason that clinicians may miss the obvious importance of this factor is that they may think they see through to the fact that the woman is serving herself through serving others. They may stress attempts to discover what she is *really* after and to show that she is just as self-serving as everyone else. It is true that women, like everyone, are motivated out of the well-springs of their own being. In that sense, we all, at bottom, act on what is moving us individually. It is also true, however, that women feel compelled to find a way to *translate* their own motivations into a means of serving others and work at this all their lives. If they can keep finding ways to do this, they are often comfortable and satisfied — and they do thereby serve others. This translation of motivation accomplishes an integration that is significantly different from the integration that society encourages in men. In fact, our society specifically discourages men from even attempting anything like this.

One woman's experience may illustrate how this integration takes place. Anne was a serious and accomplished artist. Her art was of the utmost importance to her, and she was deeply absorbed in it. She was married, had two children, and loved her husband and children. However, she came to feel that she should paint only after she had done everything possible to answer her husband's and children's needs. As a result, she painted less and less; as her life became increasingly organized around serving her family so did most of the "meaning" of her life. While she would still derive satisfaction when she did paint she had the feeling that it was a "selfish" activity, an indulgence.

Her husband died at a young age. She was devastated, not only suffering from his loss but also from the feeling that her purpose in life was gone. The only motivation that she believed "kept her going" was concern for her two children and the absolute need to support them — now financially as well as in all other ways. She found she could best earn a living by painting and teaching art, and she could now work with deep concentration; she absolutely had to do so *for* her children. Although she had to find some balance between the devotion and attention to be given directly to them and to her work, she could allow herself both. Her artistic satisfaction was no longer selfish. Eventually she came to feel a greater sense of herself *through* herself than she had felt when her life was organized around her husband and his needs.

After a few years she remarried, and once more her work was not essential financially. Again Anne could not allow herself full commitment to her art. She felt that she did not have the right to devote herself to something "just for me." Each hour given to her work had to be almost literally weighed and tested to determine whether it could be used in doing something for her husband or children. Of course, there was almost always something that needed to be done to make their lives better or fuller.

Departure of a Super-Wife

While the internal constraints that Anne felt were not easy for her to resolve, they were relatively more understandable than the complexities that the need to serve can produce in many other instances. Anne had the great advantage of knowing at least what one of her important needs and desires was. Many psychological needs are much more difficult to grasp and define. One must have the chance to carry out this search in interaction with the world and the people in it. When women are not encouraged to undertake this pursuit, when they are in fact discouraged from doing so, they have much more difficulty learning about their needs and desires.

There is, however, for women one seemingly easy way. One can divert oneself almost entirely from the difficult exploration of one's own needs and concentrate on serving other's needs. But when this happens, women often develop the belief — usually not explicitly articulated — that their own needs, even though unexamined, untested, and unexpressed, will somehow be fulfilled in return. To compound the situation, some women come to believe that others will love them (and become permanently devoted to them) *because* they are serving these others so much and so well. The tragedy here is that people do not usually love others for this reason. They may become dependent on their services, but that is different from real interest and love. In fact, if men and children become too dependent, they can come to feel trapped by their dependency and come to hate the person who is taking care of them so well. (This is one reason some men walk out on their super-wives and some children turn strongly against their super-mothers.) If women sense that they are not being loved, this reinforces their belief that others are concerned with them only because of the service they provide. They thus lose the sense that others are interested in them, in and of themselves, because of who they are. Although this is a terrible feeling, many women believe they have to settle for it, especially after being married for some time. What alternatives have they had?

Another woman's experience may illustrate some of the compounding factors. Edith grew up the model of a "perfect female"; she was well instructed by her mother in how to win and please men. She did not know how to please herself, except by finding an attractive man with good prospects. Pretty and popular, she eventually married Bert, one of her most promising suitors. She became the super-wife and super-mother and came increasingly to rest her security on the belief that she could tie all of her family to her, not because they really loved and wanted her as herself, but because they surely needed her. She did so much for them and made life so good for them, how could they not? For a long time she prided herself on how indispensable she had become to everyone. This became almost the only source of her sense of identity.

After a number of years she suffered from incomprehensible anger, agitation, and depression. Strikingly, she knew no reason for it, but had the overwhelming feeling that she had to get away from her comfortable home. She did so. She found a job at very low pay; even to get that job she had to move from her town. The only apartment she could afford was cheap and shabby. At the time, she did this only out of some desperate sense that she "had to," not knowing why at all.

No one could understand her strange behavior. In time, as she began to build a life of her own, meager as it was, she came to discover that she had developed a mounting resentment to the position of servitude in which she had lived. She had gradually accumulated the feeling that no one *knew* or cared for her and she had come to hate the people who made her feel that way. She had not been able to recognize this resentment or figure out the basis of it. This inability to find a conception, a formulation in which to state her feelings, was *the* great trap. She now saw that she had believed that her sole worth in life lay in serving others; she desperately needed some sense that she was a person in her own right. She also needed to believe that people cared about her, as that person. These needs were so pressing that she was willing to risk the loss of old relationships.

Edith might easily have been diagnosed as bizarre and self-destructive. She left a home in which she "had everything" to go to a situation in which she had nothing. She would also have been called an angry woman — she was. Because her entire past life was lived totally under the guiding needs of another, she probably would also have been labeled "excessively dependent." She could have been readily convinced that she was suffering from a combination of excess anger and excess dependency and that she should try to get over them and return to the advantages she had. Such a course would have denied the essence of her problem.

Many women do not take the action Edith did. In a similar situation they become increasingly depressed or develop other psychic or somatic symptoms. They may fall victim to so-called involutional depressions. This is particularly likely to occur when children, by their own growth and movement, show that they do not need mother any more. Women in these depressions have a great deal of anger too, although they usually find it impossible to admit it to themselves. How is one to understand such anger when children are doing only what they are supposed to do?

As it happened, Edith's husband was genuinely concerned. He sought out his wife and tried to understand and respond to her. In time Bert was able to convince her that he truly liked and loved her for what she was becoming, which was different from what she had been.

Their new relationship did not evolve quickly or easily; there remained many misperceptions and misunderstandings to thrash through. Eventually they went on together, but on a totally different basis—Bert moved to Edith's city; he changed his working pattern and social life. There were a number of factors that helped to make this alteration possible. Bert was at least able to start the process of trying to understand an event against which he had initially reacted with much violence. He also had by this time "made it" himself and was able to reduce a little the pursuit of fame and fortune that had so totally preoccupied him through all the years of the marriage; although he did feel, to some extent, that he was still "sacrificing" some of his ambitions.

Beginning of Change

Another woman, Judy, reflects a more contemporary way of reacting to a similar situation. She is younger than Edith and initially more aware of her own needs. She wants to participate fully in her children's development, but she also wants to feel that her husband shares an equal concern and devotion—that he's as concerned about them and about her as she is about him. In addition she wants to develop her own interests; she is in touch with her need to build a sense of herself based on her own motivations and abilities, not on her husband's. She recognizes that in her adolescence everything and everyone encouraged her to concentrate on forming a relationship with a man and marrying. In today's climate she is much more able to discuss some of her early marital experiences than was Edith. This ability to articulate the problem is a great help in itself. It relieves her of the necessity to wonder blindly about what is happening and prevents her from feeling that "something must be wrong with me." But it is still not enough.

Her husband, Will, a skilled worker, understands parts of the situation intellectually. He recognizes that the strictures on her are unfair and says that in a more just society she will receive equal pay for equal work. (He can even add that perhaps she will someday receive equal encouragement.) Meanwhile, however, he cannot consider giving up any of the toehold he has acquired in his work or any of the pay he receives in order to share in the responsibility for the children. What he would lose in wages at this point is greater than the amount Judy could earn. Moreover, he cannot consider the change that an alteration in his work arrangements would make in his image of himself and his standing with "the guys at the plant." There is no question that he is devoted to Judy and to his children; but it has to be strictly an "after hours" devotion, not a determinative consideration of his daily life. The thought of losing them nonetheless fills him with dread and despair.

This story illustrates the point that it is the woman who is motivated to make the just society come about. It is she who is hurting and who deeply feels the need for change; for her it is not merely an intellectual theory about justice. She must find a solution in order to live her life satisfactorily. Will "wishes he could spend more time with the kids," but Judy is impelled to make the changes she *needs*. These changes can ultimately provide for his full participation in his children's lives. At the same time, it is important to note that Judy's desires for herself include an equally potent desire to foster her children's and her husband's development.

Strange Theories About "Human Nature"

Neither Judy's nor Edith's husband wanted to hurt or deprive anyone. This was, in fact, one reason why they reacted so negatively when their wives first raised the issue of deprivation. It made them feel cruel when they never intended to be. This issue rests on a deeper point, however: In order to pursue their prescribed male identity, they had learned to close off large areas of their own sensibilities; one important area is precisely that of responsiveness to the needs of others.

It is not that men do not serve others, in fact, and in many ways. Both men in these examples do so. Bert has always thought of his scientific work as important to "mankind." Will is a strong union member, very concerned about his co-workers. The point is, however, that the need to serve others is not *central* to a man's self-image. It is a luxury he may desire or can afford *only* after he has fulfilled the primary requirements of manhood. Once he has become a man, *by other standards,* he may *choose* to serve others.

It is clear that the large element of human activity that involves doing for others has been separated off and assigned to women. When this is combined with the fact that what women do is generally not recognized, we end up with some strange theories about the nature of human nature. These strange theories are, in fact, the prevailing theories in our culture. One of these is that "mankind" is basically self-seeking, competitive, aggressive, and destructive. Such a theory overlooks the fact that millions of people (most of them women) have spent millions of hours for hundreds of years giving their utmost to millions of others. While this fact has important consequences for women, in an ultimate sense it has equally serious implications for men *and for the dominant culture's theories about the nature of human beings.* Since man is the measure of all things — and man, literally, rather than human beings — we have all tended to measure ourselves by men. Men's interpretation of the world defines and directs us all, tells us what is the nature of human nature.

To put it all very simply: all we human beings have is ourselves and each other, but clearly it is enough. We all need *both* ourselves *and* each other. Our troubles seem to come from an attempt to divide ourselves so that we force men to center around themselves and women to center around "the other." From this division both groups suffer, but in very different ways. While the division itself seems relatively simple and obvious, a number of psychological complexities follow directly from it.

One of the complexities is that the dominant group is seriously deprived of knowing what it is like to fully integrate living for oneself and for others. The man's psychological concentration and training from an early age are on the former.

He is led to believe he *must* do that or he will feel like a failure, unmanly.

The man, or the boy, in his development is psychologically deterred from incorporating serving characteristics by an easily observable fact: there are already people around who are clearly meant to serve and they are girls and women. To perform the activities these people are doing is to risk being, and being thought of, and thinking of oneself, as a woman. This has been made a terrifying prospect and has been made to constitute a major threat to masculine identity.

From what we know so far about the development of a person's fundamental sense of identity, it is linked very early with her/his sense of being a female or male person. Latest evidence suggests that by the age of about a year and a half to three years the child already "thinks" of her/himself as a sexed person, not as a generic person.[2] Thus, the threat to a boy of not being a male person — of being a "not-male" — psychologically presents him with a sense of being no person at all. We come to link our sense of existence with a sexed existence so early that we cannot even think of ourselves as simply a "person." We can only think, "I am so and so, a man," or "so and so, a woman." "If I am not John, male, as it were, I am not anyone at all." The inner sense of not existing, of losing one's sense of one's existence, of losing one's fundamental psychic bearings, is one of the most terrifying threats one can experience. But the fact is that we do not *have* to give femaleness and maleness the meanings we presently give them. Full and mutual participation in all of life, that is, in the growth and development of others and oneself does not have to be a threat to maleness. This, like many other notions, is culturally imposed.

In a very deep sense then we have created a situation in which men's allowing themselves in a primary way to be attuned to the needs of others and to serve others threatens them with being like a woman. To be like a woman is almost to be nothing. This does not mean that all men make this formulation of thought in an explicit way; most of them do not. It does mean that this is how a man is led to feel and structure his perceptions in an internal, unarticulated way.

To be attuned to and responsive to the needs of others continuously in one's development and to allow oneself to respond to these perceptions; to let this response flow; to develop ways of doing so and at the same time to express oneself and seek one's own development; to work out an integration of this two-way flow — all this does not happen for men. Instead they are deprived of this ongoing process. Men are forced to turn off those naturally responsive parts of themselves. It is not that boys are not attuned to others and that they cannot sense others' needs. It is that they are systematically encouraged to dampen their responses. They are "dis-rewarded" from doing so. To do so is feminine. It is being not a man. It is not being. It is in the realm of the inconceivable, the dreaded, that which must be avoided.

Because our image of human possibilities is built on what men have done and what men have said is possible, we have not been able to conceive of more than "man" as so far defined. We are left believing that while many people have impulses that are generous, kind, and responsive to other human beings, at bottom, they are selfish, self-seeking, and out for themselves. Self-interest, we say, is basic. But it is not *the* basic element. It is just one possibility.

We might say that one of the major issues before us as a human community is the question of how to create a way of life that includes serving others without being subservient. How are we to incorporate this *necessity* into everyone's development and outlook? As suggested at the outset, women today have a highly developed basis for this social advance. To achieve it, however, requires a new integration of the assets women already possess. To serve and yet not be subservient requires that women bring forward certain other qualities. These facets will be discussed in the following chapters.

Ego Development

Returning briefly to the psychoanalytic theory of ego development, we note that women have been said to have more "permeable ego structures" or "less rigid ego boundaries" than men. Freud, himself, said that women have a less-developed super-ego—a seeming disparagement. In theory, the ego and the super-ego develop in relation to reality (that is, reality as it is defined by one's culture) and the demands it places upon the individual. Reality makes these demands because each person is presumably to be groomed to be a living representative of his culture and its standards.

Prevailing psychoanalytic theories about women's weaker ego or super-ego may well reflect the fact that women have no ego or super-ego at all as these terms are used now. Women do not come into this picture in the way men do. They do not have the right or the requirement to be full-fledged representatives of the culture. Nor have they been granted the right to act and to judge their own actions. Both of these rights seem essential to the development of ego and super-ego as they are defined. This does not mean that women do not have organizing principles or relate to "a reality" in a particular way. But women's reality *is* rooted in the encouragement to "form" themselves into the person who will be of benefit to others. They thus see their own actions only as these actions are mediated through others. This experience begins at birth and continues through life. Out of it, women develop a psychic structuring for which the term ego, as ordinarily used, may not apply.

We are suggesting then that the organizing principle in women's lives has not been a *direct* relation to reality — as reality is culturally defined. Nor is it the mediation between one's own "drives" and that reality (which is the source of the development of the ego). Instead, women have been involved in a more complex mediation—the attempt to transform their drives into the service of another's drives; and the mediation is not directly with reality but with and through *the other person's purposes* in that reality. This self-hood was supposed to hinge ultimately on the other person's perceptions and evaluations, rather than one's own.

Such propositions are complex, and basic to them all is the very nature of one's tie to reality. The greatest part of this tie comes via other people for everyone; but for women, as we have seen, the very structuring of the relationship to other people is basically different than it is for men. Serving others is one way of describing the fundamental form in which women's ties to others are structured. However, there is an even more basic issue to be explored; it is the salience and meaning of relationships to other people in the first place. This topic will be taken up in Chapter Eight, but first it is important to interrupt briefly to discuss further the nature of reality or the "real world," as it presents itself differentially to each sex.

chapter seven

outside "The Real World"

It may seem as if I am saying that women have all the virtues and can, or should, now go out and save the world. That is certainly not the point. What I am saying is that human experience has obviously been divided in two — not down the middle, but somewhere askew of it. One moiety, the part assigned to women, has been devalued and treated almost as if it did not exist, or as only important enough for women to do. Of course, it is an "essential" part — everyone knows *someone* has to raise children, and everyone wants someone to take care of the bodily comforts and the "lower need" of sex. And every man wants someone to take care of him when he is sick or disabled.

All of these things, the things women are allowed to do, are in a significant way, removed from the life of one's time. Women's place is *outside* the ongoing action. To nurse the old, the sick, and the disabled is taking care of those who are temporarily or permanently retired; raising children is an involvement with those who are not yet in the main action. Women even take care of those who are in the main action during the hours of the day when they are out of action — that is, they provide care and comfort to the tired man when he comes home at night. Women's other role, the biological production of the next generation, is deemed essential, but it also positions them effectively outside the action of their own generation. This is one of the circumstances that women refer to when they say they feel they have lost touch with "the real world."

It is true that in many times and places women have played the major role or an equal role in the economic production of their society; but even in such societies, they have rarely, if ever, had an equal role in the *direction* of the society. In many places women were the main food growers, the major economic producers, but their place was not defined by that activity.[1] It seems that no matter what women have done, it has not been considered the valuable activity. They are still defined as the producers and caretakers of people — and doing that is less important. Certainly in our society the aspects of life that have been assigned to women have been culturally defined as inferior and separated off from "real life."

Women work with the pervasive sense that what they do does not matter as much as what men do. In this they are, of course, in absolute touch with reality — reality as defined for them by society. But by accepting the social definition they are led away from another reality, that of their own lives and experience. Men believe that what they do is more important, and in this respect they too are in touch with the socially defined reality. (Here is another sort of experience that may have been interpreted as penis envy in women. Women have felt as if men had something they did not, and they certainly did.)

Some have argued that this division of responsibility is right and good. Let women take care of these things, they say. They are essential, and someone has to do them. If someone has to be assigned to take care of life and if taking care of life is outside of the "real world," let it be women. Such a course would seem barely conceivable in a democracy. Moreover, two other extremely important points follow from our present division of life experience. First, if society deems women's areas less valuable, it cannot also tell a woman that she can, or should, feel herself to be a fully valued person; and if we do not allow a person the basic right to be a fully valued member of society, we limit the flow of her psychological expression in a million ways, large and small. The second major point is that the areas designated as women's place are *not* secondary or unimportant. Because they have been so defined, they have led to major problems for men as well as women, and the perpetuation of this division stands in the way of a solution for both sexes.

Psychoanalysis, in attempting to probe the depths of the human psyche, entered the "unreal world" of "mankind's" unsolved problems; in threading its way through the many complicated labyrinths, it did not recognize it for what it was — woman's world. What society has so far failed to see is that living contact with this world need not make you weak. It can strengthen us all.

Inside "The Real World"

Some of the things I have written may sound like things our grandmothers would have told us: "Men will be boys. We let them play their little games with each other. We know it isn't about the important things, but they think so. So we let them. We take care of them so that they can go on playing. Without us they couldn't." But the games are not fun anymore, if they ever were. Many end in war games. What grandma did not tell us is that men are capable of something altogether different. (If they are not, then perhaps women had better take over completely!) But even though men are untapped wells of potential, they will not move forward if women continue to subsidize the status quo.

There has been a deluge of recent writing in many fields in the dominant culture bemoaning men's entrapment. These writings say that the goals held out to man create a person unable to arrive at satisfaction or even a sense of connection with what he is doing and those with whom he is doing it. Witness the stream of "alienation" and "failure of communication" literature. What this writing has not seriously considered is that these difficulties relate to the subjugation of women.

All social structures that male society has built so far have included within them the suppression of other men. In other ways, too, all of our society's advances are still a very mixed blessing. What a relatively few men in our advanced society have been able to build has been at the great expense of other men. Technologically advanced society has led to vast improvements for a small group of men and some improvements for a somewhat larger group — at the expense of misery for many and the destruction of whole cultures for others.

A particular consequence of this destructiveness is that we have a very distorted image of human beings: people are out for themselves; they really want to put the other guy down. Freud's underlying assumptions are similar: man is doomed. His most basic, innate impulse — the impulse to pleasure (which, Freud said, is the source of all motivation, all life) — leads only to conquest and destruction. Society can only hope to hold this destructiveness in check and sublimate these impulses. This interpretation may follow easily from a society which has separated and assigned to one sex only the potentialities for action, decision, and power.

It is true that it is a rat race out there; it is a hard cruel world. The prospect is not very appealing. The so-called identity crisis in youth (male youth; that term does not really describe females so far) may result from not really wanting to opt for that world, not really wanting to leave behind the world — the so-called child's world — in which people are ready to help, to care, to encourage your development, to feel and to act *for* you rather than against you. This reluctance is seen by clinicians as immaturity and dependency. (Thus do things get turned on their heads.) But why indeed would today's youth want to leave the caring world and grow up? Grow up to what? Yet, on the other hand, how can one be an effective, self-directing person without being, simultaneously, an active participant and proponent of the rat race? To be less than a committed participant is to risk being less than a man.

For women, as we have shown, it need not be so. But for women, too, the issues become sharply drawn when they themselves take living in "the real world" seriously. As women attempt to use all of themselves, they face the task of putting all of their characteristics into operation under their own determination. This prospect has not existed before on a broad scale. It will require a new transformation of women's *valuable* qualities. This transformation will produce conditions vastly different from those in which women acted for the development of someone else — the real actor and real decision-maker. A new integration will be required, under new guiding principles.

As women start to define these new principles for themselves they emphasize different issues and questions. While these issues have in fact always been present in some form, they now demand a new level of conscious and concerted consideration. The next section will point to some of the issues that attain greater prominence when women seek to redefine themselves and to act on these new definitions.

It may be important to differentiate briefly this discussion from other ideas, some of them very ancient: for example, the idea of Yin and Yang, Jung's notion of the hidden woman in every man and vice versa, and David Bakan's dicussion of the opposition of agency and community.[2] In a different vein, Christopher Lasch has described a period when, in response to the first wave of feminism, it was advocated that women move into public affairs to do "social housekeeping" for the society, in order to bring their cleanliness and morality into the corrupt world.[3]

These formulations fail to take seriously the inequality of power and authority between men and women. It is hardly women's task to go into the dominant culture to "cleanse it" of its problems. This would merely be repetition in another form of "doing for others" and "cleaning" for others — now cleaning up the "body politic." Likewise, Jung's woman "hidden inside the man" is not the same as its reverse. Instead we have to ask who really runs the world and who "decides" the part of each sex that is suppressed. The notions of Jung and others deny the basic inequality and asymmetry that exists; they are also ahistorical. The question is one of what has been suppressed and what can begin to emerge at this time in our history — and who is able to bring forward the suppressed parts? Who has declared what is to be labeled masculine and feminine? Finally, these formulations are themselves a reflection of the whole dichotomization of the essentials of human experience. The present divisions and separations are, I believe, a product of culture as we have known it — that is, a culture based on a primary inequity. It is the very nature of this dichotomization that is in question.

part iii — notes in a future key

Part II emphasized certain psychological qualities that women
have developed out of life as it has been. In themselves, they do
not present a full picture even of the past; certainly, they are
not enough for the future.

Part III will point to some of the elements that emerge as
women move into their futures. These new emphases do not
arise de novo. They, too, grow out of women's specific
experience and the values that experience has engendered.

We have been carrying along as a subtheme the notion that
certain key areas in women's lives parallel the material that
psychoanalysis unearthed. This section, too, points toward
topics with which psychoanalysis and psychotherapy are constantly concerned but which they have not categorized as
essential human needs. I believe that they are essential,
although they will eventually require more precise specification
than the rough approximations suggested here. They have to
do with creativity and cooperativeness, and also with authenticity, self-determination, and power — as well as the necessity
for engaging in conflict, even as one is involved in cooperation. At this time in history, these are some (not all) of the
factors crucial for women's development.

Even before we discuss these topics, there is a most basic

element that must be considered: the nature of human ties. Psychoanalysis, in its second stage, has been constantly concerned with this subject. Like the issue of "doing for others" — but even more basically — this theme involves a fundamental organizing principle in women's lives. It has the same two-sided quality as the topics already discussed, but is even more important to consider as a keystone for women's future possibilities.

chapter eight

ties to others

Male society, by depriving women of the right to its major "bounty" — that is, development according to the male model — overlooks the fact that women's development *is* proceeding, but on another basis. One central feature is that women stay with, build on, and develop in a context of connections with others. Indeed, women's sense of self becomes very much organized around being able to make and then to maintain affiliations and relationships. Eventually, for many women the threat of disruption of connections is perceived not as just a loss of a relationship but as something closer to a total loss of self.[1]

Such psychic structuring can lay the groundwork for many problems. Depression, for example, which is related to one's sense of the loss of connection with another(s), is much more common in women, although it certainly occurs in men.

What has not been recognized is that this psychic starting point contains the possibilities for an entirely different (and more advanced) approach to living and functioning — very different, that is, from the approach fostered by the dominant culture. In it, affiliation is valued as highly as, or more highly than, self-enhancement. Moreover, it allows for the emergence of the truth: that for everyone — men as well as women — individual development proceeds *only* by means of connection. At the present time, men are not as prepared to *know* this. This proposition requires further explanation.

Let us start with some common observations and examples and then return to unravel this complex, but basic, issue.

Paula, a married woman with children, was similar in some ways to Edith, who was described in Chapter Six. Paula, too, had been raised to make a relationship with a man "who would make her happy," and she had organized her life around serving his needs. Most of her sense of identity and almost all of her sense of value rested on doing so. She believed that Bill "made her valuable," even though, in fact, she had great abilities to respond to everyone's needs while running a big household. As time went on, she felt some diminution in her central importance to Bill. As this feeling increased, she doubled her efforts to respond to and serve him and his interests, seeking to bind him to her more deeply. The actual things she did were not in themselves important to her. (In fact, she accomplished what she set out to do with great ease and efficiency.) They counted only as they produced an inner sense that Bill would be attached to her intensely and permanently, and that this, in turn, would make her worthwhile. Thus, her successful life activity did not bring satisfaction in itself; it brought satisfaction only insofar as it brought Bill's interest and concern.

When Paula's efforts did not produce the result she was after, she became depressed, although she did not know why. She was filled with feelings that she was "no good," that she "didn't matter," that "nothing mattered." She felt Bill did not care enough, but she could not document convincing evidence for this feeling. He was fulfilling his role as a husband and father according to the usual standards; in fact, he was "a better husband than most," said Paula. This factor, of course, made her feel even more "crazy." She *knew* Bill cared, but she could not *feel* that he did somehow. She became persuaded then that there must be something terribly wrong with *her*. At the same time, none of the worthwhile things she did, provided her with any satisfaction at all.

It is important to note here that Paula was not "dependent," at least in the meaning usually implied by that term. In fact, she "took care" of Bill and their children in many ways. It is rather that Paula's whole existence "depended on" Bill's word that she existed or that her existence mattered.

Paula, like many depressed patients, was a very active, effective person. But underlying her activity was an inner goal: that the significant other person — in this case Bill — must affirm and confirm her. Without his affirmation, she became immobilized, she felt like no one at all. What did it matter how she thought of herself? Such words had no meaning.

Even women who are very accomplished "in the real world" carry with them a similar sort of underlying structure. One woman, Barbara, holds a high academic appointment. In discussion she is a rigorous and independent thinker. Yet she struggles with an inner feeling that all of her accomplishment is not worthwhile unless there is another person there to make it so. For her, that other person must be a man.

Beatrice, a very successful business woman who could "sell" and persuade shrewd bargainers who intimidated many men, used to ask, "But what does it all mean if there isn't a man who cares about me?" Indeed, when there was, she found her activities alive and stimulating. When there was not, she became depressed. All of her successes became meaningless, devoid of interest. She was still the same person doing the same things but she could not "feel them" in the same way. She felt empty and worthless.

Kate, a woman who was actively working for women's development, was sophisticated in her understanding of women's situation. At certain times she would become acutely aware of her need for others and condemn herself for it. "See, I'm not so advanced at all. I'm as bad as I always was. Just like a woman."

While Barbara and Kate did not become depressed, they felt the same underlying factor operating. Depression is used here only as an illustration of one end result of this factor. There are many other negative consequences.

How Connection Works

All of the women cited offer hints of the role that affiliations with other people play for women. We see the kinds of problems that can result when all affiliations, as we have so far known them, grow out of the basic domination-subordination model.

According to psychological theory, the women discussed above might be described as "dependent" (needing others "too much") or immature in several ways (not developed past a certain early stage of separation and individuation or not having attained autonomy). I would suggest instead that while these women do face a problem, one that troubles them greatly, the problem arises from the dominant role that affiliations have been made to play in women's lives. Women are, in fact, being "punished" for making affiliations central in their lives.

We all begin life deeply attached to the people around us. Men, or boys, are encouraged to move out of this state of existence — in which they and their fate are intimately intertwined in the lives and fate of other people. Women are encouraged to remain in this state but, as they grow, to transfer their attachment to a male figure.[2]

Boys are rewarded for developing other aspects of themselves. These other factors — power or skills — gradually begin to displace some of the importance of affiliations and eventually to supersede them. There is no question that women develop and change too. In an inner way, however, the development does not displace the value accorded attachments to others. The suggestion here is that the parameters of the female's development are not the same as the male's and that the same terms do not apply. Women can be highly developed and still give great weight to affiliations.

Here again, women are geared all their lives to be the "carriers" of the basic necessity for human communion. Men can go a long distance away from fully recognizing this need because women are so groomed to "fill it in" for them. But there is another side: women are also more thoroughly prepared to move toward more advanced, more affiliative ways of living — and less wedded to the dangerous ways of the present. For example, aggression will get you somewhere in this society if you are a man; it may get you quite far indeed if you are one of the few lucky people. But if you continue to be directly aggressive, let us say in pursuit of what seem to be your rights or needs as a man, you will at some time find that it will get you into trouble too. (Other inequalities such as class and race play an important part in this picture.) However, you will probably find this out somewhat later, *after* you have already built up a belief in the efficacy of aggression; you already believe it is important to your sense of self. By then it is hard to give up the push toward aggression and the belief in its necessity. Moreover, it is still rewarded in some measure: you can find places to get some small satisfaction and applause for it, even if it is only from friends in the local bar, by identifying with the Sunday football players, or by pushing women around. To give it up altogether can seem like the final degradation and loss — loss especially of manhood, sexual identification. In fact, if events do not go your way you may be inclined to increase the aggression in the hope that you can force situations. This attempt can and often does enlarge aggression into violence, either individual or group. It is even the underlying basis of national policy, extending to the threat of war and war itself.

Instead, one can, and ultimately must, place one's faith in others, in the context of being a social being, related to other human beings, in their hands as well as one's own. Women learn very young that they must rest primarily on this faith. They cannot depend on their own individual development, achievement, or power. If they try, they are doomed to failure; they find this out early.

Men's only hope lies in affiliation, too, *but* for them it can *seem* an impediment, a loss, a danger, or at least second best. By contrast, affiliations, relationships, make women feel deeply satisfied, fulfilled, "successful," free to go on to other things.

It is not that men are not concerned about relationships, or that men do not have deep yearnings for affiliation. Indeed, this is exactly what people in the field of psychodynamics are constantly finding — evidence of these needs in men as well as in women, deep *under the surface* of social appearance. This has been said in many different ways. One common formulation states, for example, that men search all their lives for their mothers. I do not think that is is a mother *per se* that they seek. I do think men are longing for an affiliative mode of living — one that would not have to mean going back to mother if one could find a way to go on to greater human communion. Men have deprived themselves of this mode, left it with women. Most important, they have made themselves unable to really *believe* in it. It is true that the time with their mothers was the time when they could really believe in and rely on affiliation. As soon as they start to grow in the male mold, they are supposed to give up this belief and even this desire. Men are led to cast out this faith, even to condemn it in themselves, and build their lives on something else. *And they are rewarded for doing so.*

Practically everyone now bemoans Western man's sense of alienation, lack of community, and inability to find ways of organizing society for human ends. We have reached the end of the road that is built on the set of traits held out for male identity — advance at any cost, pay any price, drive out all competitors, and kill them if necessary. The opportunity for the full exercise of such manly virtues was always available only to the very few, but they were held out as goals and guidelines for all men. As men strove to define themselves by these ideas, they built their psychic organizations around this striving.

Some may believe that we had to arrive at a certain stage of "mastery" over the physical environment or a certain level of technology, to see not only the limits but the absolute danger of this kind of social organization. On the other hand, it may be that we need never have come this long route in the first place; perhaps it has been a vast, unnecessary detour. It now seems clear we have arrived at a point from which we must seek a basis of faith in connection — and not only faith but recognition that it is a requirement for the existence of human beings. The basis for what seem the absolutely essential next steps in Western history if we are to survive is already available.

A most basic social advance can emerge through women's outlook, through women putting forward women's concerns. Women have already begun to do so. Here, again, it is not a question of innate biological characteristics. It is a question of the kind of psychological structuring that is encompassed differentially by each sex at this time in our development as a society of human beings — and a question of who can offer the motivation and direction for moving on from here.

The central point here is that women's great desire for affiliation is both a fundamental strength, essential for social advance and at the same time the inevitable source of many of women's current problems. That is, while women have reached for and already found a psychic basis for a more advanced social existence, they are not able to act fully and directly on this valuable basis in a way that would allow it to flourish. Accordingly, they have not been able to cherish or even recognize this valuable strength. On the contrary, when women act on the basis of this underlying psychological motive, they are usually led into subservience. That is, the only forms of connection that have been available to women are subservient affiliations. In many instances, the search for connection can lead women to a situation that creates serious emotional problems. Many of these are then labeled neuroses and other such names.

But what is most important is to see that even so-called neuroses can, and most often do, contain within them the starting points, the searching for a more advanced form of existence. The problem has been that women have been seeking connections that are impossible to attain under the present arrangements, but in order to conduct the search women have been willing to sacrifice whole parts of themselves. And so women have concluded, as we so readily do, that we must be wrong or, in modern parlance, "sick."

The Search for Attachment — "Neuroses"

We have raised two related topics: one is social and political, the other more psychological. One is the question of how women can evolve the kinds of connections which will advance women's development and help women to build on this strength to effect real change in the real world? Secondly, until we accomplish this task — and along the way — can we understand more about the psychological events of our lives? Can we better understand why we suffer? At the very least, we may be able to stop undermining ourselves by condemning our strengths.

In the attempt to understand the situation further we can return to some of the women mentioned at the beginning of this chapter. They all expressed a common theme: the lack of ability to really value and credit their own thoughts, feelings, and actions. It is as if they have lost a full sense of satisfaction in the use of themselves and all of their own resources — or rather, never had the full right to do so in the first place. As Beatrice put it, there is the sense "that there has to be that other person there." Alone, her being and her doing do not have their full meaning; she becomes dry, empty, devoid of good feeling. It is not that Beatrice needs someone else to reflect herself back to her. (She knew she was, in fact, an excellent and accurate judge herself.) Her need seems even more basic than that. Unless there is another person present, the entire event — the thought, the feeling, the accomplishment, or whatever it may be — lacks pleasure and significance. It is not simply that she feels like half a person, lacking total satisfaction and wanting another person, but still able to take some satisfaction from her own half. It is like being no person at all — at least no person that matters. As soon as she can believe she is using herself *with* someone else and *for* someone else, her own self moves into action and seems satisfying and worthwhile.

The women referred to in this chapter are not so-called "symbiotic" or other immature types of personalities. (Such terms, incidentally, may well require re-examination in relation to women.) In fact, they are very highly developed and able people who could not possibly be categorized in such a way. Nor, on a more superficial level, do phrases like "seeking approval" or "being afraid of disapproval," really cover the situation, although these factors play a part.

Their shared belief that one needs another person in a very particular way manifests itself in different ways for different people. In one form it leads readily into depression. The experiences of the women described here may thus provide some further clues to depression, may help us understand some aspects of it. While Paula and Beatrice did suffer depression, for other women there are different manifestations.

Everyone in the various psychological fields would probably readily admit that we do not fully understand depression (or fully understand anything else for that matter). Depression, in general, seems to relate to feeling blocked, unable to do or get what one wants. The question is: what is it that one really wants? Here we find difficult and complicated depressions that do not seem to "make sense." On the surface it may even seem that a person has what she wants. It often turns out, however, that, instead, she has what she has been led to believe she should want. (For many young middle-class women it was the house in the suburbs, a nice husband, and children.) How then to discover what one is really after? And why does one feel so useless and hopeless?

Beatrice's experience may offer some understanding on this point. She eventually said that she sought to bind the important other person to her absolutely, and she wanted a guarantee of that bond. She was anything but a passive, dependent, or helpless woman; but all of her activity was directed to this goal, which she believed she needed to attain. While she did not really need *that* kind of relationship, she was not convinced of it internally. (Often her activity in search of this goal took on a very forceful and manipulative character. Although the goal was usually pursued covertly and obscured from herself, it was felt very distinctly by those around her.)

Beatrice had developed the inner belief that everything she does feels right *only* if she does it for that other person, not for herself. Above all, she had lost the sense that the fulfillment of her needs or desires could *ever* bring her satisfaction. It is almost as if she had lost the inner "system" that registers events and tells her whether they make *her* happy or satisfied. The "registering" of what feels like satisfaction has shifted; it now comes only through her sense that she can make the other person remain in a particular kind of relationship to her. Only then can she feel strong and good. (In more complex depressions, like Beatrice's, it may not be the other person *per se* that one desires to bind but the image of the *kind* of relationship one believes one needs. For example, women whose children have grown up may not want to retain the individual children but they feel they must have the mother-child kind of relationship. In fact, one may not really need such a relationship; but the belief is strong, and a person who has spent a long time organizing her psyche on that basis will not easily relinquish the idea. Further, she has long since lost the belief that she can really have any other kind of relationship.)

Another facet of Beatrice's problem was the large amount of anger generated. To compound the problem, like many other women, she had great difficulty in allowing herself to express her own wrath. She did, however, become furious if the other person did anything that seemed to threaten to alter the bond. It seems clear that being in such a position is very conducive to rage. How could she not get angry at that other person to whom she had given so much control over her life? But Beatrice would become even more depressed because she interpreted her anger as an added sign of her unworthiness. In spite of her deep unhappiness, she could not really believe that there was any other possible way to live.

Like Beatrice, people liable to depression are often very active, very forceful; but the activity must be conceived of as benefiting others. Furthermore, it is organized around a single pursuit — seeking affiliation in the only form that seems possible: "I will do anything if only you will let me stay in this kind of relationship to you."

Some other aspects of depression may help to explain these points. It has long been recognized that there are so-called paradoxical depressions, which are most often observed in men. They occur after a man who has been competent receives a promotion or other advance that presumably should make him happy and even more effective. Such depressions may reflect the fact that the individual is forced to admit to increased self-determination and to admit that he, himself, is responsible for what happens. He is not doing it for someone else or under the direction of someone else. Women do not get promotion depressions so commonly because they do not get many pro-

motions. Nonetheless, in Beatrice, who could accomplish pro-
digious feats as long as she had at least one person in a position
superior to her, a very similar dynamic was at work. She would
absolutely never let herself have the top job, although several
had been offered to her.

A similar process may be at work in a phenomenon seen in
psychoanalysis. It has long been recognized that people sometimes have what are called "negative therapeutic reactions."
This means that they make a major gain and then seem to get
worse after it. Bonime has suggested that many of these reactions are in fact depressions and that they occur when a person has made a major step toward taking on responsibility
and direction in her/his own life.[3] The person has seen that
she/he can move out of a position of inability and can exert
effective action in her/his own behalf, but then becomes
frightened of the implications of that new vision; for example, it would mean the person really doesn't need the old
dependent form of relationships. She/he then pulls back
and refuses to follow through on the new course. Such re-
treats occur in men as well as women, but for women this
situation is an old story, very similar to what goes on in life.

The significance for women of these two examples may be
this: "If I can bring myself to admit that I can take on the determination and direction of my own life rather than give it
over to others, can I exist with safety? With satisfaction? And
who will ever love me, or even tolerate me, if I do that?" Only
after these questions are confronted, at least to some degree,
can one begin to ask the even more basic question: what do I
really want? And this question, too, will not always be answered
easily. Most women have been led too far from thinking in
those terms. It often takes strenuous exploration, but usually it
turns out that there are deeply felt needs that are not being met
at all. Only then can one begin to evaluate these desires and to
see the possibility of acting to bring about their attainment;
and only then does one realize that there can be satisfaction
in such a course. Moreover, it then becomes apparent that
one does not need or want the kind of binding one believed
was so essential.[4] Since the process described in this para-

graph is so often thwarted, it seems obvious why women are set up for depression.[5]

Many complications come in to compound the situation for women, as they did for Beatrice. If one believes that safety and satisfaction lie in relationships structured in particular kinds of bonds, then one keeps trying to push people and situations into these forms. Thus, Beatrice was constantly working very actively at getting a man into this kind of relationship. She had a program for action, the only one she was able to construct, but the program created her own bondage. This is why psychological troubles are the worst kind of slavery — one becomes enlisted in creating one's own enslavement — one uses so much of one's own energies to create one's own defeat.

All forms of oppression encourage people to enlist in their own enslavement. For women, especially, this enlistment inevitably takes psychological forms and often ends in being called neuroses and other such things. (Men, too, suffer psychological troubles, as we all know; and the dynamic for them is related, but it *does* take a different path.)

In this sense, psychological problems are not so much caused by the unconscious as by deprivations of full consciousness. If we had paths to more valid consciousness all along through life, if we had more accurate terms in which to conceptualize (at each age level) what was happening, if we had more access to the emotions produced, and if we had ways of knowing our own true options — if we had all these things, we could make better programs for action. Lacking full consciousness, we create out of what is available. For women only distorted conceptions about what is happening and what a person can and should be have been provided. (The conceptions available for men may be judged as even more distorted. The possible programs for action and the subsequent dynamic are, however, different.)

Even the very words, the terms in which we conceptualize, reflect the prevailing consciousness — not necessarily the truth about what is happening. This is true in the culture at large and in psychological theory too. We need a terminology that is not based on inappropriate carryovers from men's situation. Even a word like *autonomy,* which many of us have used and liked, may need revamping for women. It carries the implication — and for women therefore the threat — that one should be able to pay the price of giving up affiliations in order to become a separate and self-directed individual. In reality, when women have struggled through to develop themselves as strong, independent individuals they did, and do, threaten many relationships, relationships in which the other person will not tolerate a self-directed woman. But, when men are autonomous, there is no reason to think that their relationships will be threatened. On the contrary, there is reason to believe that self-development will win them relationships. Others—usually women—will rally to them and support them in their efforts, and other men will respect and admire them. Since women have to face very different consequences, the word *autonomy* seems possibly dangerous; it is a word derived from men's development, not women's.

There is a further sense in which the automatic transfer of a concept like autonomy as a goal for women can cause problems. Women are quite validly seeking something more complete than autonomy as it is defined for men, a fuller not a lesser ability to encompass relationships to others, simultaneous with the fullest development of oneself. Thus, many of our terms need re-examination.

Many women have now moved on to determine the nature of their connections, and to decide for themselves with whom they will make relationships. As soon as they attempt this step, they find the societal forms standing in opposition. In fact, they are already outside the old social forms looking for new ones. But, they do not feel like misfits, wrong again, but like seekers. To be in this unfamiliar position is not always comfortable, but it is not wholly uncomfortable either — and indeed it begins to bring its own *new* and different rewards. Here, even on the most immediate level, women now find a community of other seekers, others who are engaged in this pursuit. No one can undertake this formidable task alone. (Therapy, even if we knew how to do it in some near perfect way — which we do not — is not enough.)

It is extremely important to recognize that the pull toward connection that women feel in themselves is not wrong or backward; women need not add to the condemnation of themselves. On the contrary, we can recognize this pull as the basic strength it is. We can also begin to choose relationships that foster mutual growth. In the following chapter we will discuss such instances.

Other questions are equally hard. How do we conceive of a society organized so that it permits both the development and the mutuality of all people? And how do we get there? How do women move from a powerless and devalued position to fully valued effectiveness? How do we get the power to do this, even if we do not want or need power to control or submerge others? It would be difficult enough if we started from zero, but we do not. We start from a position in which others have power and do not hesitate to use it. Even if they do not consciously use it against women, all they have to do is remain in the position of dominance, keep doing what they are doing, and nothing will change. The women's qualities that I believe are ultimately, and at all times, valuable and essential are not the ones that make for power in the world as it is now. How then can we use these strengths to enhance our effectiveness rather than let them divert us from action?

One part of the answer seems clear already. Women will not advance except by joining together in cooperative action. What has not been as clear is that no other group, so far, has had the benefit of women's leadership, the advantage of women's deep and special strengths. Most of these strengths have been hidden in this culture, and hidden from women themselves. I have been emphasizing one of these strengths — *the* very strength that is most important for concerted group action. Unlike other groups, women do not *need* to set affiliation and strength in opposition one against the other. We can readily integrate the two, search for more and better ways to use connections to enhance strength — and strength to enhance connections.

For women to derive strength from relationships, then, clearly requires a transformation and restructuring of the nature of relationships. The first essential new ingredients in this process are self-determination and the power to make the self-determination a reality. But even before getting to this major issue, there are questions facing many women: "If I want self-determination, what is it I really want to determine? What do I want? Who am I anyhow?" The difficulty of answering these questions has sometimes served to discourage women. The discouragement occurs even in women who are convinced that there is something deeply wrong with the old way. Given the history that women's lives have been so totally focused on others, it is easy to see that such questions bear a special cogency and come from a particularly hidden place in women. In the next chapter, we will explore this question under the general heading of authenticity.

It is important here to note that this discussion of the importance of relationships for women is by no means exhaustive. Nor is it a full discussion of any of the related, complicated problems, such as depression. Rather, it is an attempt to unravel a topic that requires much new examination. I hope that it will give rise to further discussion.

chapter nine

becoming oneself— authenticity, creativity

For women, as for certain other groups of people, being oneself — authenticity — was hardly spoken of seriously until recently, although it figured prominently in the concerns of members of the dominant culture. Authenticity and subordination are totally incompatible. But a tendency peculiar to men's view of authenticity has obscured the fact that relationships can lead to more, rather than less, authenticity. We can illustrate this by following the experience of a woman, Jane, a mother and factory worker who had previously been on welfare. Shorter fragments from other women's lives will suggest the common themes in this topic in the midst of the individual women's diversity.

> Now I feel I have a center that is myself. I can tell when I act out of that kind of feeling, as opposed to the other [the past way of feeling and acting]. It's still hard, but when I act out of that center it's a very different feeling.

Her statement summarized a long story. It began when she

took a new and significant step: she began to deal directly and honestly with the people at work.

Jane had been accumulating a store of criticism and anger at her women co-workers in the factory. Seeing a widening gulf between herself and them, she finally took courage in hand and tried to tell one of the women what she thought. This was the first time she had expressed such troubling feelings to anyone. Looking back at it, she described the experience:

> I realized I was really scared to death to tell this woman directly that I was angry at her. I hadn't known that. I've never bothered with women before. I always thought men were best to be with. I got along with them. Men were easy. You never had to deal with them directly. I could always hide out under the "woman thing" with them. I knew how to play the game. There was a safety in it.
>
> Oh, I know men liked me because of my looks. It boosted their egos to have the good looking girl. I always knew I was pretty, usually the prettiest girl around, and I could almost always get the man I wanted.
>
> I thought women were sappy. I was always pleasant with men too, good fun, always agreeable. If it ever came to any difference with a man, I'd back down fast. That backing down part was no act. I always had that deep scared part of me that made me feel I must be wrong anyhow no matter what. So I never really was threatening to a man; he never had to worry about me.
>
> It was different with women. You couldn't hide out and use all that game with women. So I just ignored them. They didn't matter anyhow.
>
> Now I have this center that I know is myself. But I really wonder. Can men take a woman who acts out of that center? Joe can't. [Her boyfriend at the time]. Not a man who is so shaky under all the tough front and the bluster. Maybe someone who has a sense of himself and is in pretty good shape. But you know, I'm no great social critic, but I don't see very many people like that around.

The beginnings of an increased feeling of authenticity may be seen in a seemingly small incident in the life of Doris, a woman who was at a very different point in life than Jane. She was a lawyer, as was her husband. They worked together, and most observers would have agreed that they were both extremely competent. If anything, Doris was seen as the "strong one." In addition to her job, she took care of almost everything at home and helped her husband over rough spots. A great part of her strength came from the fact that she was "emotional." When something troubled her, she seemed able to get in touch with her feelings, express them, and end up in a fairly good position to understand the situation and how she might best deal with it. While she did not always feel able to deal with her boss or colleagues in such forthright fashion, after "she got it out at home," she could usually figure out a way to handle almost any situation. Lately, however, Doris had begun to feel that her husband barely tolerated her expressiveness, that he treated her with condescension — although he never expressed this attitude in words. This especially rankled her since she believed that she carried him in many ways.

One evening after she had had a particularly hard day with her colleagues, she was telling her husband about how upset she was:

> He listened for about ten minutes. That's about his limit. Then he said, "Aw, don't let the bastards upset you." That's just the sort of thing I suspect. It sounds fine and even supportive. But it really means, "Shut up. I've heard enough." I usually drop it there. But this time, I couldn't. After stewing quite a while, I told him what I thought. At first, he made excuses, "It was just getting late." He even said some complimentary things like, "I was just trying to say that 'Of course, you were right.'" That would have been another place to drop it easily. But I told him I thought they were excuses; that I thought he meant he can't take my thrashing around in my feelings like that.
>
> After about ten minutes he admitted it, "Yeah, I had heard enough." Even that was a big improvement, because it's hard for him to rescind anything he once says. He likes to

be always right; so it's very hard for him to admit that much. Then we talked a lot about it. And somehow the whole thing got straightened out. I felt fine and was able to get some sleep. [One of Doris' problems had been insomnia.]

In the past this sort of thing always gave me a sort of permission to go around feeling mistreated. I'd sulk for a few days, feel abused, even self-righteous. Oh, not so anyone else would know, just to him. He'd get some kind of message and start being very good to me after a few days, and things would seem all right again. But the matter itself was never opened up. This time I didn't end up feeling self-righteous. It was much better than being self-righteous.

[The following dialogue took place between Doris and me.]

"How did you feel when you did that?"

"Scared. Very scared."

"Of what?"

"Of his anger."

"That all?"

"I know what you want me to say — of my own anger. But I don't think you're right. I know pretty well when I'm angry; so I can tell you I was just plain scared of his anger. You're like the rest of them. People always think I'm so strong I wouldn't be afraid of his anger. I just was scared of his anger. That was the real feeling. The only other thing, maybe, was something I thought of afterwards — it didn't hit me on the spot — was I'm also scared of feeling myself as not strong and in control. That is the picture everyone seems to want of me. And I seem to need to uphold it for myself; I see that. I sure didn't feel in control then at all. You won't believe it, my heart was pounding. But I see I don't have to always keep up that false pretense."

Another woman, Nora, spoke to a similar theme. In some ways the context was especially hard for her because it was in her women's group, a group which had newly come to mean a great deal to her. It was a group in which there was a high level of unity and good feeling. Nora had gradually come to realize, however, that the group saw her as the strong one. When she wanted to express some of her real anguish, they tended "not to let me"; they brushed it off or downplayed it with such comments as, "Oh, you'll handle it well," or "You're so good at that." Nora sensed that they needed to see her as strong for their own reasons, but she was more and more unwilling to accept this false and one-dimensional view of herself. It doubled the difficulty she already experienced in exposing her more desperate feelings. Finally, she managed to express this part of herself only by shouting, "You're not letting me talk. You're not hearing me. I don't care what you need! You've got to hear what I'm saying!" Nora's shouting revealed her initial difficulties in broaching the issue, but she was able to explain what she was afraid of:

> Anger, my own anger. I never in my life acted like that. [I was afraid of] their anger too. But more than that, sort of the fear that they'd all collapse or something. Like I was betraying them, letting them down. They needed to have the image of a strong woman so much. I'd always felt I had to keep up the image of a strong person, even as a kid — for my family you know. Now, here it was again.
>
> But I guess the need to really be myself and to have them know me was stronger by this time. And I think, too, I was feeling, "If I'm not going to fight to be myself, here, in this group, I'll never do it." Anyhow, the great thing was that they didn't collapse. That was the big lesson for me. For them, too, I think in the end.

Authenticity Through Cooperation

Jane, the first woman described here, suffered from a deep-seated feeling that she could never make her desires heard by anyone and that she could never effect anything, make anything come about. No one, she thought, would respond to her. "I couldn't reach anybody when it really mattered to me, and there was nothing I could do that would really make any difference." These feelings *are* terrifying. Jane's had their origin in a family in which her few attempts at expression were not only ineffective, but produced an onslaught by her parents. Her father had an overwhelming temper. Her mother's form of attack was "hysterics," often ending in what appeared to Jane to be total collapse — screaming, crying, taking to her bed, getting some sickness, saying she wished she were dead, that she was dying, and so on.

Jane's story illustrates the potential strength that often is hidden inside a facade of weakness. She appeared to be, in fact she described herself as, a weak woman clinging to a strong man. Seemingly paradoxically, she deeply feared weakness, which to her meant the image of her mother, flailing about, hysterical, obviously miserable but never able to do anything to make a real change in her life. Jane dreaded becoming this woman; she hoped to avoid it at all costs. But her path to a strength greater than her mother's could not be direct; it had to be through attachment to a strong man who would "do it all for her." Nothing in her upbringing or in society encouraged her to act on her own behalf or build a sense of her own effectiveness. Like some other women, she said once, "If only I had seen my mother be strong — even once. If only I had had a glimpse of that as a *possibility* for me."

The problem was that Jane saw only one alternative to the helpless, dependent person, the person she dreaded being. That was the totally strong, self-sufficient person who was freed forever from weakness or neediness, and, most of all, from the *effects of other people*. It was, in short, her image of a man. Men, she thought, could be immune to these dreaded feelings. But the slightest hint of being like a man was, of course, totally unacceptable.

Instead, she attached herself to men but remained afraid and alone with these feelings. In her isolation, nothing entered to change her deep-seated feelings of weakness and fear, until she made the move toward her co-workers. Finally, Jane spoke to one of the women, Blanche. She told her that she didn't think she (Blanche) and some of the other women were doing their jobs properly. And this, she said, made it harder for her, and it made her angry. Blanche became angry in return. Accusing Jane of being a snob, she made it clear that all the other women thought so also. Jane did not care about them; why should they worry about her? This accusation suggests that the women were probably accurately perceiving Jane's contempt for them, her belief that women were "sappy" and her aloofness that came from her fear of getting involved with them.

But after the angry exchange, Blanche was able to say, "I'm glad you brought it up. I couldn't have done it myself, but I've been very upset over you."

The significant point here is the genuine strength in Blanche's response. She expressed approval for Jane's raising a difficult topic and admitted to her own deficiencies. Even her candid complaints about Jane carried a message of respect and true engagement. Each of the women criticized the other quite honestly, and while all disputes and negative feelings were by no means cleared away immediately, the ability to turn to each other to deal with problems was begun.

A few of the other women at the factory subsequently aired their irritations and anger. While for Jane the situation was fearful and awkward at first, in time the candor flowed with more ease and even some humor. After that, the women in this group gradually developed an amazingly supportive relationship; they knew each other's weaknesses, and they spoke directly about them. They spent much less of their energies in defending themselves against each other. Most important, they turned to each other through many difficult times involving not only the factory but their home lives as well.

Jane is overwhelmingly grateful to her friends and has received so much help from these relationships that she feels impelled to help the other women whenever she can. As she has come to know some of the women and the burdens they bear, she marvels at their strengths. One woman supports several children alone; another has a fatally ill child; a third, a mentally defective child.

Isolation

All the foregoing growth and understanding was not accomplished easily and quickly. Jane was involved in some serious intervening struggles, both with her co-workers and her own tendencies. Not the least of these struggles came with Jane's discovery that she sought power and strength too — just like everyone else. She had attempted to maintain a sense of power over women and, thereby, keep them from hurting her. Her methods were dismissal and contempt; it was easy to put down and ignore women. Moreover, Jane had an alliance with the "winners," that is, men. This alliance allowed Jane an inner, but fraudulent, sense of power and "pride." She was not openly aware of her own desire for power or her *use* of power until she became involved with her co-workers. Until then she was predominantly aware of feelings of failure and needing men.

Jane found that she could admit to her dreadful feelings of weakness only after she learned that she could *do* something about them, that is, only when she developed some real belief in her capability. She found that as she continued to admit to them with more honesty she could also continue to deal with them more effectively. This sequence has since become an ongoing and reinforcing process.

This account may seem to have almost a storybook ending, but it is true. A great deal of the outcome hung on the ability of the other women to respond so forthrightly and well. In fact, differences still exist. The women do not share an identical outlook, but they can accept their differences and meet on direct terms. Jane works hard at her two jobs, factory worker and mother. She has setbacks and real troubles with which to contend. It is, however, she says, "as if everything had a different feel to it. It's me." I think what she is talking about is authenticity.

The important factors are two: Jane found her *own* path to effective action for herself; and she found this via turning to others. These factors now reinforce each other. All the while that Jane appeared dependent and clinging, she was deeply alone and isolated. Paradoxical as it may seem, she was trying to go it alone, playing her female counterpart of the "immune male." By allowing herself to engage with others, she found she could be effective for herself. She moved on to greater strength, but she moved on as part of the process of turning to other people. She is simultaneously much stronger herself and more able to rest her faith more strongly in others. In a certain sense, to persevere with her old isolation took a lot of strength; but it was strength that simultaneously undermined her. Now she believes absolutely in her need for other people. In fact, she has pleasure in finding that people "can do this for me." At the same time she has a greatly enhanced sense of her own personal effectiveness.

Sexual Authenticity

What about Jane's relationships with men during this time? For a period — when she was not yet certain whether she was really acting "from her center" or complying in the old way — she felt relations with men could be confusing. Interestingly, some of the most puzzling times were the "good times" when she could easily agree with a man. She was not yet sure if she could believe in her agreeableness. Was she falling into the old easy game?

At a later point, she met a man who seemed to really enjoy the "new parts" of her. She was more certain that she no longer "tailored her version of things to fit" what she thought a man was after; it was up to him to either like it or not. So far, it seems he does. Jane thinks she may really like him, but she is not sure yet. There is still a lot to find out and to work out for herself about how she has to be and wants to be. He may turn out not to be the kind of person she wants in a relationship.

There is the sexual question, too. In the past Jane had felt that "only strong men turned me on." As her whole psychic outlook shifted and the idea of the strong man was losing its former salience, she wondered whether anybody would attract her sexually. By the time sex came into the picture, however, the feared problem dissolved without a great deal of trouble.

Perhaps it is accurate to say that Jane's sense of the meaning of strength took on different connotations and assumed a different place in the whole picture. She no longer has a compulsive concern with the sterotypic strong man, but she certainly is interested in men who have their own strengths. She has been able to be freer and more sexually involved with a man who knows both her strengths and vulnerabilities and who is likewise able to share with her the varied sides of himself.

Another woman, Emily, was also developing a sense of her own center, through a process somewhat like Jane's. She, too, enjoyed acting "like herself" honestly and directly and was finding the experience a great new source of energy. She, too, eventually met men who seemed to respond to her "new self." But as soon as she became sexually involved with them, she began to lose her sense of her self. "I can almost physically feel it going. I slip back into an old passive mold. I don't have anything to say about what's happening. It's just happening *to me*."

There are several dimensions to this problem. One involves accepting her own sexuality and allowing herself sexual pleasure. This problem is compounded by old feelings that sex is immoral and dirty. (Such feelings are still very much with us even in these days of sexual revolution.) If a woman, even unwillingly, still thinks of sex as bad, then it is sometimes easier to engage in it (to even enjoy it) if she can maintain the concept that it is the man's doing. She is just complying, and it's "really for him." This attitude is part of the history of what women were supposed to do and feel. But it does not match what Emily now wants, and achieves, in other areas.

For Emily, there is an additional dimension to the sexual question. To be herself in sexual engagement is for her the final confirmation that her "new self" really *exists*. It will "prove," as it were, that she really can be the person she is glimpsing now. It will allow her to tap all of her suppressed energies and direct them toward her goals. It will be, in a sense, "dependency's end," and she is not quite ready to face it. It seems frightening but it is also "too good to be true." (It also means she is still asking a man to prove that her new self exists — to give it his stamp of validation via the final test, his demonstration of sexual interest.)

For a while, the experience of feeling herself thrown back into the old mold tended to turn Emily against sex and to discourage her. Eventually, when she was able to further sort out these issues for herself, she no longer required the man, or even sex itself, to prove that her "new self" did indeed exist; further, that it was all right for it to exist. Instead, sex could be *one* expression of her own total self and of her feelings. Emily is now willing and able to say that she takes a firm hand in directing herself, and she can now decide if it is all right, in sexual situations as in all others, to let her fuller self exist and flourish. She has moved another large step away from demanding that the man do this for her — via sexual confirmation.

Jane, on the other hand, faces a different step at this time. She knows that her new relationship may bring added difficulties. If she comes to like and love this man there will be a greater temptation to give to him, to do for him. These things will come very easily to her.

> It may be harder then to know if I am acting out of myself or not. The very feeling of wanting to do things for him can add to the confusion. I want to do things for him, but I want to know *why* I am doing them — whether it's to *avoid* being myself or because it *is* being myself.

Sometimes she thinks she may have to postpone any serious relationship with a man until she can be even clearer about her own motives. Then there are days when she feels surer of herself, and she says:

> I think I sometimes get the two mixed up, but pretty soon I can get back to knowing whether I am acting out of that center of myself. When I feel I'm not, I can find the ways to get back to it.

First Steps

Many women today find themselves in a situation similar to Jane's at the beginning. She knew what she did not want — to get caught in another relationship like her previous marriage to one of her "strong men" who failed her. At the same time, she thought she "had to have somebody else in order to live."

By this she meant a man — one who would not disappoint her. But she certainly did not know what she, herself, wanted. This is not so strange when we consider that a woman's whole conditioning is contrary to seriously finding out what she wants.

Today, the lack of a definite desire is, in itself, very discouraging for many women. It ultimately represents one kind of "copout," although an understandable one. If you do not know what you want, you can avoid taking the risk to get it; for women this is a serious risk. But to say this, alone, is not very helpful. Women find they have to begin to explore their own thoughts and feelings, whatever these are, and wherever they must begin.

Initially in this process, women often discover many feelings that do not seem to make much sense. It is very hard to tolerate feelings and thoughts that one cannot fit into an acceptable framework of concepts. This experience immediately calls for one kind of creativity, a making and remaking of ways of thinking and stating a multitude of previously unacceptable and unthinkable things, a topic that will be discussed further toward the end of this chapter. Alternatively, many women initially experience "only negative feelings" — anger, resentment, hatred, and the like. They often add further criticism to themselves because they believe their feelings are ill-founded. It is very important to see these feelings as often appropriate and necessary. Anger can be one of the first authentic reactions. While it is not pleasant in the traditional sense, it may give its own kind of pleasure because of its undeniable, hard reality. It can be a mobilizing and strengthening factor, although eventually women can add others to it. (Given the opposition women face it is not a one-time experience by any means, but an emotion which may be validly called forth repeatedly.)[1]

All of these points of likely discouragement are important as examples of the kinds of things women encounter. While by no means the complete list, they are some of the common feelings that women face as they start on their path toward authenticity.

Risks. Each of the women in our examples had to take a large risk — a risk that was particularly difficult for her, even though it may not seem so to others. These kinds of risk have some components that are common to most women. Each woman had to risk focusing on her own desires and needs, even if it meant — as it so often can appear to mean — displeasing others. Often the important *other* is the person in whom her major emotional attachment is invested. If it is the male partner, her whole economic livelihood and social status are usually involved as well.

As soon as many women think of incurring somone else's displeasure — especially a man's — they equate it with abandonment. The risk, in its psychic meaning and impact, becomes the risk of abandonment and condemnation. (The woman will be left, because *she* was wrong and bad.) But whether the man would, in fact, leave or not, women are conditioned to feel he will. For women this is often one of the greatest and most frightening risks. In some cases the man does not, in fact, leave as the woman pursues her course; in others, the woman, herself, leaves and perhaps finds better relationships altogether. But the crucial factor is that she must take the initial risk — as a psychological step. If women avoid taking this risk, in most cases they cannot begin the journey. It is only when the woman can move to thinking about the true quality of her connections and how to improve or change them rather than thinking of first pleasing another and conforming to his desires and expectations that she can even begin to know herself. With the economic and psychological realities today, this risk is still huge.

The sense of pleasing herself has been a very rare experience for most women. When they attain it, it is a newfound joy. Women often go on to create enhancing relationships, but if their goal is to secure the relationship *first*, they usually cannot find the beginning of the path. This, I believe, is because male-female relationships have been so effectively structured to deflect women away from their own reactions and fulfillment. In the past this deflection had set in almost automatically, even before a liaison had been formed.

In addition to "pleasing myself," another part of the pleasure that Jane and other women are experiencing is a much greater freedom both to be themselves and to "allow," and even enjoy, other people being themselves. When one acts on this basis one need neither exploit others nor put excess demands on them to be a certain kind of person. Instead, one can be more freely oneself in the midst of intense engagement with others.

Doris and her husband offer a small example of this reciprocating freedom. When he means "shut up," he now says, "shut up" — and then Doris argues with him, rather than "allowing him to feel big and strong and right." They both have laid aside the elaborate, indirect procedures by which they used to carefully control and restrict each other. They can appreciate and enjoy each other more because they no longer try to force each other into certain positions.

Creativity with a Place to Go

Personal creativity is a factor of supreme importance, which we have probably barely begun to appreciate. One exciting aspect of the current ferment by women is the fact that as they struggle for authenticity, they simultaneously illuminate their personal creativity. In so doing they elucidate the creativity that struggles on in a more hidden way in all people at all times.

Personal creativity is a continuous process of bringing forth a changing vision of oneself, and of oneself in relation to the world. Out of this creation each person determines her/his next step and is motivated to take that next step. This vision must undergo repeated change and re-creation. Through childhood and adulthood, too, there are inevitable physical changes as one grows and then ages. These demand a change in one's relation to the world. Further, there are the continuous psychological changes that lead to more experience, more perceptions, more emotions, and more thought. It is necessary to integrate all these into a coherent and constantly enlarging conception of one's life.

Each person repeatedly puts together a conceptualization that has never been put together before — that is, one constantly creates a personal vision. Despite all our commonality, each of us, each day, creates our own particular attempt to put the picture together, as it were. It is never exactly the same as anyone else's, and it is never the same as the one we made yesterday. That is, we each repeatedly re-confront the necessity to "break up the gestalt," as Max Wertheimer has described it.[2] At best, our conceptions will be an accurate reflection of what we have experienced and how we feel and think about the experience. The closer we can come to this ideal of authenticity, the better off we are. And the more we can act in terms of our own conceptions, the more whole and authentic we feel. Having acted, we can go back and "correct" our conceptions about the world, about ourselves, about what we want.

It is true that the very ways we find to conceptualize experience are in large measure given to us by the culture in which we learn "how to think and feel," or even learn what thinking and feeling are. But people are also continually straining against the boundaries of their culture — against the limiting categories given by that culture — and seeking the means to understand and to express the many experiences for which it does not suffice. This is true for all people. For women today it is a preeminent factor. As we have seen, there are fundamental reasons why women do not easily find the means at hand to express and conceptualize their experience. But they are struggling to develop these means. In this way, too, women's current endeavor can more clearly illuminate the hidden mental events that go on in all people.

It is certainly true that throughout history economic conditions have forced (and continue to force) most people into a life of drudgery. It is also true that even in the most oppressive conditions the human mind is constantly at work, giving meanings to it all, trying to make it understandable. The mind does not seem to be, in today's parlance, "a closed system," but rather a system capable of infinite enlargement. The closer the mind can connect with what one is actually experiencing the better its inherent creativity can flourish. The more opportunity we have to put our mental creations into action, the more comprehensively we can, in turn, feel and think. One builds on the other.

The exciting and enlightening impact of the women's experiences we have discussed can be appreciated when we realize that they are on the cutting edge of a new and larger vision. Their personal creativity is an absolute necessity in the attempt to find a way to live *now*. The women, who are finding a way to deal with their own intensely felt experience, are at the same time creating a more general new vision of womanhood. For this vision to flourish, they and other women will have to create new social institutions to support and enlarge it. It is precisely at such points that one sees that the real motivation for a new form of living arises today in women out of intensely felt personal needs. The ways of achieving this new form of living will likewise have to be women's ways; to achieve ways of living that will attend to all women's needs, the forms inevitably will have to include more mutuality, cooperation, and connection, on both a personal and a larger social scale.

We have not dealt here with women who are particularly advanced in their sense of who they are and what they want. In fact, there are women today who are outstanding in their ability to act on the basis of their own perceptions and evaluations, who are already far along the road to creating a new way of living. Such women have a strong conviction of their own worth and of their own right to self-development and authenticity. Some have a background of high accomplishment; others have a strong sense of fighting for a valuable cause. The attempt here has been to get at the underlying forces affecting all women as a group, the nodal points from which forward movement can spring. The events in the lives of specific women are examples in the attempt to talk about these forces. Part of the reasons for doing so, however, is the hope of demonstrating that the *need* for authenticity and creativity do not belong only to the advanced, the educated, or the elite. These forces are played out in different forms for women in differing circumstances, but they are necessities for all of us.

In our time we have heard a great deal about people's lack of authenticity. What we cannot hear so clearly is that, for half of the population, the attempt at authenticity requires a clear and direct risk. For women to act and react out of their own being is

to fly in the face of their appointed definition and their prescribed way of living. To move toward authenticity, then, also
involves creation, in an immediate and pressing personal way.
The whole fabric of one's life begins to change, and one sees it
in a new light. As one woman put it, "I keep seeing everything
with a different meaning now. Most days I feel as if I'm ad-
libbing my way through. I don't follow the script I used to
know." For this new and much more intense personal creating
there are no certain guideposts. There are often anguish and
anxiety, but there are also clear satisfactions and joys along
the way, even long before there is anything like a sense of
completion.

chapter ten

all this, but not enough

"Power" is almost a dirty word — in somewhat the same way "sex" has been. For women especially it has been an unmentionable subject. But all the strengths discussed in the preceding chapters will remain "unreal," and unrealized, if women do not have the power to put them into effective operation. To do so, they will have to acquire economic, political, and social power and authority. At present women wield virtually none.

The strategy and tactics for effective action on the economic and political fronts require extensive analysis and debate, and that effort is being carried forward in many places. Concomitant with it, we need to raise the question of the nature and psychological meaning of power and self-determination, lest we misconstrue both women's advantages and liabilities for this struggle. The words "power" and "self-determination" have acquired certain connotations, that is, they imply certain modes of behavior more typical of men than women. But it may be that these modes are not necessary or essential to their meaning. Like all the concepts and actions of a dominant group, "power" may have been distorted and skewed. It has rested almost solely in the hands of people who have lived with a constant need to maintain an irrational dominance; and in their hands it has acquired overtones of tyranny. Similarly, the idea of self-determination, for dominant groups, has been built on a base that included, *pari passu,* the restriction of another group. This is not self-determination in a pure state but a concept that has acquired connotations extrinsic to its real nature — signs of another, hidden, process.

It is important then to look into some of the meanings of power and self-determination to see whether, as women struggle in the economic, political, and other fields, they can redefine power and self-determination.

Power

In general, for women today, power may be defined as "the capacity to implement." A large part of this task is the implementation of the abilities women have already. There is also a need to implement the new ones women are developing. This has not been the meaning of "power" in the past. Power has generally meant the ability to advance oneself and, simultaneously, to control, limit, and if possible, destroy the power of others. That is, power, so far, has had at least two components: power *for* oneself and power *over* others. (There is an important distinction between the ability to influence others and the power to control and restrict them.) The history of power struggles as we have known them has been on these grounds. The power of another person, or group of people, was generally seen as dangerous. You had to control them or they would control you. But in the realm of human development, this is not a valid formulation. Quite the reverse. In a basic sense, the greater the development of each individual the more able, more effective, and less needy of limiting or restricting others she or he will be. This is not the way things have been made to appear.[1]

Women do not come from a background of membership in a group that believed it needed subordinates. Also, women do not have a history of believing that their power is necessary for the maintenance of self-image. Women, however, do have their own kinds of problems with power. Women's inexperience in using all of their powers openly, combined with past fears of power, is now taking on new forms. As women move into greater activity and scope, they face new kinds of power struggles and rivalries. Most women are not practiced in the forms and conventions by which men have been geared for rivalries since childhood. (Jane, for example, avoided open power struggles with members of either sex.) Women's feelings can be particularly raw in these realms, and some situations can be very discouraging.

Yet these struggles cannot be leapt over. They are important areas for women's attention, and some may make serious mistakes in the course of dealing with them. There are new factors however. Women have created forms for the more open and cooperative examination of both their desires and deficiencies in these realms. Many women can more readily turn to others in hopes of dealing with these areas. They can use their abilities to support each other, even as they develop more effective and appropriate ways of dealing with power — sorting out its appropriate use and reacting to its inappropriate use in themselves and others.

The issues of power have to be faced; there are conflicting forces among women themselves. Most of all, it is important to sustain the understanding that women do not need to diminish other women; therefore women do not need to take on the destructive attributes which are not necessarily a part of effective power, but were merely a part of maintaining a dominant-subordinate system. Women need the power to advance their own development, but they do not "need" the power to limit the development of others.

Women start, however, from a position in which they have been dominated. To move out of that position requires a power base from which to make even the first step, that is, to resist attempts to control and limit them. And women need to move on from this first step to more power — the power to make full development possible. This is important to stress. Dominant groups tend to characterize even subordinates' initial small resistance to dominant control as demands for an excessive amount of power! (For example, today, when subordinates take even the first step by refusing to bring the office coffee, they may be treated as if they now had power over the boss.)

There is another way in which power, as we have seen it work so far, has been distorted. It has operated without the special values women can bring to it. Indeed, these womanly qualities have seemed to have no bearing on the "realities" of power in the world. I am not suggesting that women should soften or ameliorate power — but instead that, by their participation, women can strengthen its appropriate operation. Women can bring more power to power by using it when needed and not using it as a poor substitute for other things — like cooperation. We can then begin to open up closed assumptions.[2] The goal is, eventually, a new integration of the whole area of effective power and womanly strengths as we are seeking to define them.[3]

Self-Determination

Women come from a position in which their own nature was defined for them by others. Their selves were almost totally determined by what the dominant culture believed it needed from women and therefore induced women to try to be. As indicated at the outset of this book, such definitions by a dominant group are inevitably false. Further, as indicated all through this work, such definitions are grossly distorted by the dominants' own unresolved problems and dilemmas. These definitions then are far removed from women's "real nature"; certainly they do not reflect what women seek to become as self-determining individuals. To begin to define themselves almost "from scratch" and to discover what it is they want is a vast undertaking for everyone.

Power is, of course, intimately linked to this venture. Without the power to put such determinations into action, women will continue to lead circumscribed lives controlled by others — those least able to make valid determinations.

Here, too, as with all of the previous topics, the prior terms of discussion may be inadequate and skewed. Moreover, they can be traps. For example, it is certainly oppressive for women to be dependent economically, politically, socially, and psychologically. However, the simple opposite, to be what is called "independent" in the dominant group's conception of that term, may be a spurious goal. Perhaps there are better goals than "independence" as that word has been defined. Or, rather, there may exist better conditions, which the word itself tends to deny: for example, feeling effective and free along with feeling intense connections with other people.

Self-determination can be a significant concept only *if* it begins where women begin. At the same time, understanding where women are, in itself, changes and enlarges the meaning of the term, adding the special views of women. These views can help in the effort to attain self-determination, instead of diverting women into possibly spurious directions — even frightening ones like the so-called independence of the male — that may not be valid definitions in any case. Indeed, women's induced fear of their own power and self-determination has been so ingrained that it requires closer examination. Exploration of this fear, itself, may provide important clues to the routes to greater self-determination and power.

Women's Fear of Power

Male society as it has been so far constituted is afraid of women's self-directed effectiveness. A suggestion of how frightening this prospect is occurs when women talk about women's power rather than women's effectiveness. Because men are afraid, they have induced fear in women. But the dynamic is very different in each sex. It is important to separate these. Women certainly do not have the same reasons for fear that men believe they have, but it is *made to seem* that they should.

We have all heard the terms "castrating woman," "bitch," and the like. They have been enough to deter many a woman, not only from aggression but even from mere straightforward assertion. But we must ask, who created these terms? Out of whose experience did they originate?

The reasons for male fear of women are many, and they range from the superficial to the very deep, intermingled all along the way. As I have suggested, when women begin to move out of their restricted place, they threaten men in a very profound sense with the need to reintegrate many of the essentials of human development — the essentials that women have been carrying for the total society. Those things have been warded off and become doubly fearful because they look as if they will entrap men in "emotions," weakness, sexuality, vulnerability, helplessness, the need for care, and other unsolved areas. At a more obvious level, women's self-directed effectiveness will quite readily lead to the obvious need to reexamine many supports, including cheap labor, that women have provided so readily.

On the other hand, what are the reasons women fear their own power? In the first place, women's direct use of their own powers in their own interests frequently brings a severely negative reaction from the man. This in itself has often been enough to dissuade a member of a dependent group from using her own power directly. Because of experiences of this sort, many women have developed an exaggerated inner equation: the effective use of their own power means that they are wrong, even destructive. Furthermore, this message is conveyed to girls from early childhood, even before they have a chance to test it in their own lives. Is it surprising, therefore, that women have developed an inner sense that their effective and direct use of themselves must be destructive of someone else? In fact, the way women's lives are arranged, and considering the things that women are supposed to be doing for others, current reality has a good chance of seeming to confirm this conception for them. Acting for oneself is made to seem like depriving others or hurting them. This is, for example, how Anne, the artist discussed in Chapter Six, thought of her painting. While Anne could see this conception operating, she said it was still hard "to really get it out of my head." The same reaction took on much more complex features in several of the other women described earlier.

Jane, the woman discussed in the last chapter, described a fear that obstructed even the first precondition of power. She, herself, had made the decision to move to this city in the belief that it might lead to better things. When discussing the fact that this decision had had good results, she said:

Stop. I don't want to hear that. That makes me scared . . . It's even frightening for me to think that I really did make that decision and that it turned out *right* . . . That really is frightening if I let myself *feel* it. I never decided anything for myself. There was always this feeling that I wouldn't make a right decision. Of course, I don't *really* know what to do; I sort of fell into everything . . . But even if I did decide something, I don't want to know about it. If I let myself think I decided it, I made it happen — and it turned out *good* — I feel anxious, like right now.

It means I really do *know* that I can figure things out . . . Then it really gets down [to the fact] that it might be right for me to know something. You don't know how frightening that is. You don't understand that. If I have any basis for believing [that] I know what's good for me, then it becomes much harder . . .

Jane's attempt to deceive herself reveals the intense anxiety she felt about this initial step in using her own powers. It is important to recall, however, that Jane had been driven to try to gain almost absolute power indirectly. She was never effective, she never achieved it, but she forcefully clung to that approach nonetheless.

Another woman, Frances, was at a different stage in the process of taking on more open power and self-determination. Although a very active and able person, she would not let herself know about her capacities. In talking about the past, she said:

When Sam [her husband] was there I had confidence, and I had much less fear about failing at things. I seemed able to move and make things happen. The possibilities were open. When he left, it felt as if everything had closed down. It seemed as if things wouldn't come out right. I'd fail at them. I was afraid to even start on anything. Somehow when he was there, things could happen. It was as if he made them happen.

I see now that I did most of them. I even thought of most

of them, but it never seemed that way. It seemed as if he were doing them.

Now I've changed all that. I *know* I make things happen.

Funny thing. Now he wants to come back and it all looks the reverse. It looks as if things will shut down. They will—if I go back in the old way. It'll all be his doing and I'll be "powerless" again. The old system had to center around our both seeing it all that way, and acting as if it all came from him. I don't need to see it that way anymore. I see now, that he needed to. He still does. But at that time I somehow did too.

It became evident that some of Frances's feeling of hopelessness had stemmed from her fear of recognizing that she had powers; that she could and did make things happen, and that it would be safe to do so. At first, she had brushed aside any suggestion that she undertake something by herself, for herself: "Just for me? If it's just for me, what's the point? That just doesn't feel like any reason at all." There — in a nutshell — is woman's strength and woman's problem.

Masochism and Power

It is around the issue of power that certain aspects of so-called feminine masochism revolve. Jane illustrates why it can sometimes seem much easier to be, and remain, the victim than to struggle for oneself. For even in a situation that is objectively destructive, the victim does not have to confront her own desires to change the situation, her own power to do so, nor the anger that has mounted and accumulated over her victimized position. It can seem easier to blame the other person and thus protect oneself from dealing with these difficult issues. Since society so firmly encourages women to remain in this position, moving out of it means working against very heavy odds. To attempt to change the situation threatens women with no place to go, no alternatives, and, worst of all, total isolation and complete condemnation. Such threats can be well validated by reality, then recycled to reconfirm women's already deeply internalized fears.

Anger is an especially important part of powerlessness. Remaining in a powerless position can be a refuge from one's fearsome anger. Recognizing and feeling anger is initially very frightening. If one has felt powerless for a long time, one has often reacted with anger. (People do not merely accept such things; they always react to them.) Even women who now want to be openly assertive can get caught in the fear of being angry, which they often don't want to be. It is frequently hard to separate the anger from the assertiveness. Sometimes, too, women are afraid that the degree of their anger is excessive or unjustified. Usually one can learn how to separate the two only if one allows oneself the right to test and explore the anger. Moreover, a great deal more of the anger may be justified than one allows oneself to admit. Sometimes truly blaming the person(s) who hurt you can seem much harder than continuing the masochistic circle of self-condemnation. This is especially, and tragically, true if one believes that the other person is absolutely necessary to one's very existence. A "masochistic person" may *seem* to blame the oppressor; but she blames herself even more, and the situation is never changed for either person.

Power and Non-Power Realms of Life

For women trying to build their own lives or struggling with work and families, all of the womanly strengths mentioned earlier may seem of little help and no comfort. How do they help women to better their lives? They are not the characteristics that help one to "make it" in the world as constituted. Exactly so; that is the very point. All of these characteristics can be seen as valuable *only* as they are also seen in a dynamic state, in motion toward something more. Indeed, for many women today, it seems that these are the very tendencies they must struggle hardest to get away from if they are to act for themselves. There are very important times when some women feel they have to steel themselves against these characteristics if they are going to get anywhere at all, or escape from a particular personal bind.

It seems to me that, at these times, the characteristics themselves are not trapping women or holding them back; it is rather the *use* to which the abilities are put and the clear fact that as soon as one acts on the basis of them one is easily led into subservience, lack of dignity, and lack of freedom. It need not be so, and the additions of power and self-determination are the two determining factors. But it can still be very difficult to sort out the conflicting personal strands. At times in one's life it may seem necessary to throw over much of the "package" because dignity or the need to represent oneself authentically is the order of the day — the essential next step in order to do anything or to escape from a bind that is immobilizing. On the individual level, each woman must start from her particular place in life. However, a perspective on the larger possibilities may help in understanding the many individual variations.

All of the valuable qualities mentioned earlier — like participating in the development of others — will not get you to the top at General Motors, were that path open to women. They will not even provide you with a self-determined, authentic, effective life. Indeed, the point is that the characteristics most highly developed in women and perhaps most essential to human beings are *the* very characteristics that are specifically dysfunctional for success in the world as it is. That is obviously no accident. They may, however, be the important ones for making the world different. The acquisition of real power is not antithetical to these valuable characteristics. It is a necessity for their full and undistorted unfolding.

It is clear that as women now seek real power, they face serious conflict. Conflict, both in society and as an area of study in psychology, has been seen as a particularly troublesome element. It is important to examine it further, for conflict, too, is not necessarily what it has been made to appear.

chapter eleven
reclaiming conflict

Conflict has been a taboo area for women and for key reasons. Women were supposed to be the quintessential accommodators, mediators, the adapters, and soothers. Yet conflict is a necessity if women are to build for the future.

All of us, but women especially, are taught to see conflict as something frightening and evil. These connotations have been assigned by the dominant group and have obscured the necessity for conflict. Even more crucially, they obscure the fundamental nature of reality — the fact that, in its most basic sense, conflict is inevitable, the source of all growth, and an absolute necessity if one is to be alive.

As women learn to make use of conflict, they will accomplish two major tasks: first, they will escape the trap of the "rigged" conflict — one conducted solely in terms set by others, terms that guarantee that women will lose. Simultaneously, they will illuminate the understanding that conflict is an inevitable fact of life and is not bad by any means.

I have stated that the dominant group's attempt to ignore and deny the existence of certain crucial unsolved conflicts and problems has led it to use women as convenient depositories of these aspects of life. (I am referring here to the societal level, although this is certainly true on the most intimate personal level as well.) In doing so, a dominant group tends to say that "things are what they are" and that "what they are, is right." What psychoanalysts found, instead, is that things are *not* what they are said to be. They are expressions of conflict and attempts at resolution. Whatever "is" originated in conflict and continues to operate in conflict. The important questions are: what really causes conflict, and have we accurately formulated the terms of the conflict?

The major initial psychoanalytic discovery was that symptoms are not what they seem — they are not fixed and static. For example, a hysterical paralysis is not *like* a physical paralysis. It is not a paralysis in any sense of the term. It is, or it expresses, an attempt to move when movement, for important reasons, is simultaneously blocked. This "paralysis" is a *process* of conflict, not a "thing" or even a static state of being. It is in motion and therefore capable of change.

The fact of the existence of conflict is the point of emphasis here. Not only are symptoms the embodiment of conflict; all of life is too. Put simply, the big secret that psychoanalysis found — and it is basic to all of its other secrets — is the secret of conflict itself.

As women seek self-definition and self-determination, they will, perforce, illuminate, on a broad new scale, the existence of conflict as a basic process of existence. As long as women were used in a massive attempt to suppress certain fundamental human conflicts, the basic process of conflict itself remained obscure. As women move out of that position, conflict can become known and therefore available for more appropriate attention — with much greater hope of eventually understanding our minds. That is, women are not *creating* conflict; they are exposing the fact that conflict exists. Here again, we must start with an attempt to redefine some of the terms to which we have become accustomed.

In addition to these general and somewhat abstract levels, there are concrete conflicts that women face today economically, socially, and politically. This is blazingly clear. Precisely because women face such grinding everyday conflicts as soon as they try to move ahead, they are better able to open up the more difficult abstract levels. Members of the dominant group can more easily avoid knowledge of the existence of conflict. Women's present ability to recognize the *necessity* for conflict if they are to pursue their self-defined self-interest can therefore be a first, great, primary source of strength — a strength that women can take into their own hands and use. The second great source of strength can be the possibility — again, one that the dominant group cannot so easily grasp — that the *conduct* of conflict does not have to be the way it has been. That is, the methods of conducting conflict do not have to be those we have always known. There can be others.

Suppressed Conflict

In earlier chapters it was suggested that as soon as a group attains dominance it tends inevitably to produce a situation of conflict and that it also, simultaneously, seeks to suppress conflict. Moreover, subordinates who accept the dominants' conception of them as passive and malleable do not *openly* engage in conflict. Conflict occurs between dominants and subordinates, but it is forced underground. Such covert conflict is distorted and saturated with destructive force. Knowing only the pain and futility of hidden conflict, one believes that *that* is what conflict *is*.

It is not practically useful, however, to urge subordinates to conduct open conflict on the personal level as if they were not dependent and powerless. Women as a group, therefore, have been able to conduct almost nothing but indirect conflict until they could begin to act from a base of strength "in the real world." It is practically impossible to initiate open conflict when you are totally dependent on the other person or group for the basic material and psychological means of existence. Moreover, because women's lives have been tied to biology and childrearing, there have been additional major obstacles in the path of gaining economic and social power and authority. Obviously, such role definitions need not keep women from full participation in the world; but to change this situation requires major reorganization of our institutions and the paths to power in them. It is easy to devise work schedules and arrangements that will allow both women and men to share in childrearing and fully participate in the life of our time, if both desire to do so. But to bring these about for any large number of people will require more changes in social and economic arrangements than other oppressed groups have had to accomplish. It requires us to ask, not how can women fit into, and advance in, the institutions as organized for men, but how should these institutions be reorganized so as to include women. For example, the question is still asked of women: "How do you propose to answer the need for child care?" That is an obvious attempt to structure conflict in the old terms. The questions are rather: "If we *as a human community want* children, how does the total society propose to provide for them? How can it provide for them in such a way that women do not have to suffer or forfeit other forms of participation and power? How does society propose to organize so that men can benefit from equal participation in child care?" Obviously none of these major changes will come about without opposition. But it is most important to define the overall goals and to debate on that basis rather than be diverted into fighting on false terms.

The fact that such necessary changes seem still so far off and so radically different can serve as another possible source of discouragement. Also, women find it difficult to believe they have the *right* to ask for so much. They are *not* irrational or immoderate demands. It is important to ask instead why the provision for such clear and obvious women's needs can still *seem* like so much to ask. It is necessary therefore to reconsider some of the more basic dimensions of conflict.

The Crucible of Conflict

Conflict begins at the moment of birth. The infant, and then the child, immediately and continually initiates conflict around its desires. The older participant in this interaction approaches the infant bringing along her/his state of psychological organization, filled with a history of conceptions about what she/he wants to do, and she/he should do, what the result should be, and so on. As these two people, with two very different states of psychological organization and desires, interact, the outcome will be the creation of a new state in each person. The result will also be somewhat different from what either of them "intended." (Of course, the infant doesn't consciously "intend," but she/he has real and important purposes that she/he is pursuing.) As a result of the interaction, both parties will change, but each in different ways and at a different rate. Out of a myriad of such interactions — *conflicts* repeated over and over and in slightly different ways — each person develops a new conception of what she/he is. This continually new conception in turn forms a subsequent new desire; new action will flow from the new desire. This is conflict as the term is used here. Both parties approach the interaction with different intents and goals, and each will be forced to change her/his intent and goals as a result of the interaction — that is, as a result of the conflict.

Ideally, the new intent and goals will be larger and richer each time, rather than more restricted and cramped. That is, each party should perceive more, and want *more* as a result of each engagement and have more resources with which to act. All too often, the opposite is true, and conflicts result in *lowered* goals and diminution of resources.

Productive conflict can include a feeling of change, expansion, joy. It may at times have to involve anguish and pain, too; but even these are different from the feelings involved in destructive or blocked conflict. Destructive conflict calls forth the conviction that one cannot possibly "win" or, more accurately, that nothing can really change or enlarge. It often involves a feeling that one must move away from one's deeply felt motives, that one is losing the connection with one's most importantly held desires and needs.

Children and young people gradually come to "know" that it is dangerous to initiate conflict. Adults have been well schooled in suppressing conflict but not in conducting constructive conflict. Adults don't know enough about how to enter into it with integrity and respect and with some degree of confidence and hope. It is hardly surprising then that many conflicts turn out badly, leaving adults with anguish and fear of conflict, which children are quick to sense.

This basic difficulty with conflict, which underlies the problems encountered in handling any specific conflict, bears a strong resemblance to the way conflict is viewed and conducted by any dominant group in an unequal situation. It is important then to look at how conflict has been viewed and conducted on the larger scene — and why it has been so hard to put it on a productive base.

Old Views and Forms of Conflicts

If we ask how can we move toward putting conflict on a productive basis, it is important to recognize that this ability is not one that anyone has learned well in our society, nor in many others. We have only relatively recently emerged from a state in which conflict was barely tolerated at all. There was absolute rule and severe penalties for those who did not comply. Today conflicts between various groups in male society are still carried out on an extremely frightening and dangerous basis.

Within this context, conflict itself can appear threatening and destructive. It is more likely, however, that it becomes dangerous when its necessity has been suppressed. It then tends to explode in an extreme form — on the societal and on the individual level. This tendency of conflict, when suppressed, to turn toward violence, acts as a massive deterrent to subordinates. Conflict is made to look as if it *always* appears in the image of extremity, whereas, in fact, it is actually the lack of recognition of the need for conflict and provision of appropriate forms for it that lead to danger. This ultimate destructive form is frightening, but it is also *not* conflict. It is almost the reverse; it is the end result of the attempt to avoid and suppress conflict.

In addition to this massive psychological deterrent, there is the bedrock fact that in any situation in the real world the dominants have most of the real power. This, too, obviously is a powerful deterrent. But even with these two strong general deterrents against conflict, it is still important to ask why, in particular, do not women move ahead as rapidly and as well as they can. An important factor is the unwillingness to initiate conflict.

Initiating Conflict

For a woman, even to *feel* conflict with anyone, and particularly but not only with men, has meant that something is wrong with her "psychologically" since one is supposed to "get along" if one is "all right." The initial sensing of conflict then becomes an almost immediate proof that she is wrong and moreover "abnormal." Some of women's best impulses and sources of energy are thus nipped in the bud. The overwhelming pressure is for women to believe they must be wrong: they are to blame, there must be something very wrong with *them.*

Instead, we would assert that when women *feel* in conflict, there is often a good reason to believe they should *be* in conflict. This, at least, can help at the start. Women's energies and hopes will not be drained before they even begin to flow. In the past, women lived under a framework of conceptions and prescriptions that was destructive of them. They were attempting to fit themselves into a model of behavior that did not fit anyone; then they blamed themselves if they could not squeeze into it, or if they even felt conflicted in the process. (Men too have sensed, in their own way, that they are attempting to be "fit in an unfit fitness," as Kenneth Burke said, but the specific misfitting is very different for each sex.)

Moving from these generalizations to some of the specifics of women today, we can return briefly to Jane, Doris, and Nora, the women whose search for self-knowledge and self-directed action we reviewed in earlier chapters. Each of them faced a particular personal obstacle in her path, and in order to take the next step, each had to initiate conflict. For Doris it was with her husband, for Nora it was with the women in her women's group, and for Jane it was her co-workers.

Each woman demonstrated yet a further dimension to the initiation of conflict, for each also had to initiate conflict with the old image of herself, the image she believed she needed. This was equally as hard as handling conflict with others. Doris and Nora had an image of themselves as the consistently "strong woman" that was not valid or necessary. Jane saw herself as the weak, clinging woman. In each case, the images constituted blocks to fuller development; they stood in the way of gaining greater true strength.

Waging Good Conflict

We have suggested that moving to the new, developing further, brings conflict all along the way. There will inevitably be conflict with one's own old level of consciousness — in the broadest sense. In the midst of such a process, we have an absolute need for other people. Nora, for example, could not have understood her old images by herself. She needed other people with whom to share and to take risks, people to trust (or with whom to begin building a basis of trust, since trust does not come all at once).

Further, as one attempts to develop in opposition to the prevailing framework of the dominant culture, it is difficult to be certain that one is perceiving things clearly. It is not easy to believe one is right and, more basically, that one *has* rights. For all this, a community of like-minded people is essential.

In the past, probably the greatest threat facing women at the hint of conflict was the threat of condemnation and isolation — most of all isolation. (For anyone, this is probably the ultimate weapon but, as we have seen so often, the situation was structured so that for women it appeared *most imminent.*) Women have already constructed supportive environments to help overcome this threat. Certainly, all of us need as much help as we can get. It is difficult to see one's way all alone, to have a true vision about which aspects of conflict are appropriate or inappropriate, to know when we have the right to ask or assert and when we are making exaggerated or distorted demands.

It is not an easy or straightforward path. Meanings change along the way and are influenced by the course of the conflict itself. Who can clearly and directly know her own needs at all times? More often they emerge unclearly. Especially, if they are important, they may be highly charged with emotion and difficult to discern. To undertake such conflict in the first place requires courage. The hope for success lies in respectful engagement with other people. Until now women were encouraged to stop before they started; they did not have to be told they had little chance of winning, and even less hope of respectful engagement. All this can now be different. Women have begun to create the environment in which they can engage in respectful interaction and in real conflict.

Conflict Among Women Today

Since the first edition of this book, people have become more aware of conflicts among women precisely because women are trying to act in new ways and to enter new places in society. Conflicts have occurred over women's roles in the workplace, about issues in political organizations, over women grappling with issues of power and competition, over issues of sexual preference, over class and race, over trying to live old relationships in new ways, and a number of other topics. The seeds of these conflicts always existed, but the conflicts did not always surface. Conflict becomes more obvious when people try to do new things; they are breaking up old patterns.

Even as women struggle with today's conflicts, we can recognize that the major models we have known for conducting conflict are those derived from the dominant-subordinate mode under which we have all grown up and lived. Experiencing conflict within that mode has restricted our abilities to understand and deal with it.

Simultaneously, however, women have practiced another model, one which differs from the dominant-subordinate mode. For example, in families and in other relationships, women have tried to interact with other people in ways which foster everyone's development. This model does not operate on the basis of gaining power over others or on winning or on a zero-sum game. Women do not always succeed in this endeavor, but they usually try very hard. Women also experience pleasure in mutually enhancing interactions and the gratification that they have enlarged the lives of others rather than diminished them. In general, women desire to transfer their experiences of acting in this model to the new spheres of activity which they are entering.

Acting in a life-enhancing way in families is not easy because families have been structured on the dominant-subordinate model. Many women, however, have acquired great skill in attending to everyone's experience even while acting within a model of basic inequality. In this context, mutually enhancing interactions cannot flourish fully, but women are in familiar territory.

When women move into more institutions and organizations in society, they find a different configuration of factors. Some women have found ways to carry over to workplaces and organizations their cooperative ways of acting. In other instances, women have run into difficulty when faced with the forces operating in public settings.

We need new models for dealing with conflict within institutions and organizations and we do not yet have them. Many women are concentrating on this difficult task, trying to learn from the experiences and also the mistakes of recent years. For example, the women of the Women's Self-Help Network of North Vancouver Island in Canada have produced a series of handbooks and manuals analyzing the experience of work and conflict in a women's organization and offering guides for action. This group is making one of the most concerted and creative attempts to face these tough issues.[1]

In the present time of transition, women sometimes expect more from other women than they would from a man and then feel more disappointment and anger when these expectations are not fulfilled. At the same time, some women are giving up their role as subordinates. They act more directly and openly, especially with other women. This change is a good one. Women have been well trained to behave submissively to men, male bosses, or leaders and in some situations they can still easily defer to or comply with men. With women, however, they feel more able to recognize and state disagreements. This ability to express disagreement can lead to better relationships. Because the conflict becomes overt, people can confront it in a more fruitful fashion. However, the greater openness can be misinterpreted initially as increased conflict.

More open and direct ways of acting with others are still new experiences for women. In the past, many women acted destructively toward other women and competed with each other. Those competitions often centered around men and the accoutrements of the wife-mother role, such as having the best house or the smartest children. Conflicts were not conducted in the more honest manner which many women now desire.

Because women are trying to act in ways in which they do not have long practice, conflicts can feel raw and searing. Men have an etiquette by which they operate in conflict with other men. For example, in some public settings in certain professions, men of high standing introduce each other with great praise even when they don't believe what they're saying. They create a kind of reciprocity with the understanding that each will bolster the public image of the other. Behind the scenes, they may compete viciously and conduct power maneuvers to gain ascendancy over other men. At certain times, they form alliances based on well-calculated estimates of the power each has to trade. Many know and anticipate these ways of behaving and have been well trained in playing these games. Women typically are not allowed into such games. More important, many women do not desire to engage in them.

Women do not yet have well-developed forms by which we understand and support each other while simultaneously dealing with conflicts. If we don't want to engage in the types of power games that men play, then we have to create our own ways of expressing conflict without allowing it to be destructive. Until we develop better ways, the basic dominant-subordinate mode can reappear. Some ·women still try to imitate the dominant group by gaining status and power at the expense of subordinates, often, now, other women. Understanding such tendencies can be difficult, particularly when they occur in women who profess devotion to women's causes. Is an individual woman (or group of women) trying to build rightful strength for herself and for other women or is she trying to gain personal power at the expense of others; or is it some combination of both?

Some women may still try to mimic the dominant group by finding gross or subtle ways to dissociate themselves from women. The forms for doing this range from making themselves more powerful than other women to becoming distinctive in some way. For example, professional women can emphasize their professional status as a means of distancing themselves from "just women"; they use individual distinctions to try to escape from being a woman, a second-class person.

Other dilemmas emerge as women's groups become better established. In the early years of a group or organization, women often find great joy in coming together and sharing so many previously unspoken feelings and thoughts. Women understand and support each other. Trouble can arise when women begin to recognize their differing experiences and perceptions. They can fear losing the connections and unity which they so cherish. They can also fear that the emergence of differences will re-create a dominant-subordinate situation. Any difference can appear as threatening and as a signal that some people are "better" or superior and others are lesser.

Some women's organizations have overcome these fears, but most of us need much more practice in learning to truly value differences. As stated at the outset of this book, our society and other societies are unable to encompass difference, indeed, to value and cherish difference as the source of hope and growth for all of us. Difference comes to mean "better" and "worse."

Differences are a source of strength for each of us — so long as they are not used against us. We all have a long history of learning to fear difference. Difference has been made to be the source of power for some and the source of destruction for others. Further, particular characteristics, such as those based on class, race, gender, or even an individual ability (such as an ability which may allow access to a profession), have been used to define the total person.

Whatever abilities (or good fortune) anyone may have, each person also has her or his limitations and deficiencies. As we are each inevitably limited as individuals, so we each truly need others. It is still hard to admit this reality. This fear of difference springs from the dominant-subordinate tradition in which difference means deficiency — and deficiency is the organizing principle. As subordinates we are told we are deficient — a falsity. Then the alleged deficiencies are used against us. Meanwhile, dominants uphold the pretense that they do not have deficiencies — another falsity. Everyone becomes terrified of difference because it means deficiency. At bottom, it means being "like a woman" rather than a full-fledged person.

Within a basic dominant-subordinate context, differences of class and race compound all situations. In the last decade, women have addressed more thoroughly the complex questions of class, race, and gender.[2] Discussion and debate continue about which of these factors is most salient as well as most oppressive and also about whether this is even the appropriate question. Women who are doubly or triply oppressed by race, class, and gender have spoken out forcefully on these issues both nationally and internationally. White advantaged women have understood more about the many ways in which they benefit at the expense of minority, working-class, and poor women. They eat food and have clothes and many other basic necessities supplied by people working for subsistence wages, many of them women. In some organizations, women of differing classes and races have built a much better framework for acting together while valuing differences. These women have often engaged in hard struggles, which continue, but on new and better levels than in the past.

Differences between lesbian and heterosexual women

create conflicts in other dimensions. In one sense, sexual preference has not formed the overt basis for societal structuring of economic and social advantage in the way class and race have. In another sense, lesbian women by their very existence challenge the fundamental structure of women's dependence on men. Therefore, lesbians often have been the most viciously oppressed women,[3] and women have often been among the oppressors. In recent decades, lesbian women have raised the consciousness of all women. Lesbian writers and artists have keenly analyzed all women's situation and have created a whole new body of artistic work.[4] In women's organizations, struggles between lesbian and heterosexual women have often been painful. Here, too, some groupings of women have moved beyond the early stages of these struggles and found new ways to honor each other.

In addition to differences which spring from major social forces, women face other, interpersonal conflicts. Women may not always like other women because of their individual styles, enthusiasms, preferences, forms of humor, and the like. Of course, each woman does not have to like and enjoy all other women. Many women are developing a new spirit of appreciation of themselves and other women, recognizing the need for women to have a variety of ways of being themselves and being with others. This spirit is very different from evaluating and judging other women along narrow lines and ranking their worth by these judgments. Today we may forget how treacherous the past was. Women were drawn into harsh judgments about other women often based on such external factors as how well dressed she was, whether and whom she married, or how many children she had. These tendencies stem too from the basic dominant-subordinate situation. Subordinates are encouraged to engage in these judgmental actions against each other. Many women have moved far away from such destructive traps.

Some psychoanalytically oriented writers have suggested that the whole problem of conflict between women results from conflict in the mother-daughter relationship. In general, such an assessment uses psychoanalysis in a reduction-ist way. We readily can find psychoanalytic explanations for anything. And such explanations can become a new version of mother-blaming, which has had a long history in psychoanalysis.[5]

It is easier to blame mothers than to comprehend the entire system that has restricted women. It is true that mothers have interacted most with daughters and, thus, were the most direct agents of an oppressive system. But mothers were themselves victims of the system.

It is interesting to note that many working-class and minority women do not blame their mothers in the way white middle-class women do. Perhaps it is easier to perceive one's mother as a victim if one has seen her scrub floors or work in a factory and be grossly abused by a boss. Additionally, many minority and working-class women have seen their mothers act as strong women even in the face of oppressive conditions, and they do not condemn their mothers for being weak or succumbing to victimization. Thus, the total configuration of forces is often very different in different ethnic and class groups.

All of this is not to deny that many mothers have failed their daughters, as they have been failed by the society in which they live. In a system which so totally constricted women, mothers could not possibly give their daughters what the daughters needed, as they did not receive what they needed as mothers. But it is also true that the manner in which mothers relate to children (and adults, too) may be the only model we have of a new way of living — a model based on fostering the other person's development. Mothers have struggled to find ways to interact with children which enhance children's growth. However, no one has been attending to what mothers really need. Mothers have been deprived and devalued and conscripted as agents of a system that diminished all women. Daughters have felt the confusing repercussions of all of these forces. Further, it is impossible to analyze the mother-daughter relationship without an analysis of the actions of the father, more accurately an analysis of the overall context which defines the family structure.

Mothers and daughters' conflicts today have taken new and sometimes heightened forms precisely because many women are trying to construct their personhood in ways different from their mothers' ways — indeed, many mothers are trying to change their own lives to undo the very constraints they imposed on their daughters. Simultaneously, many mothers and daughters are developing new ways of relating to each other. Some have worked hard at this and have realized particularly poignant relationships because of the new depths of understanding they have reached about the forces impinging on them both.

These are only a few of the ways in which women experience conflict with other women. Many of the conflicts are symptoms of transition, of the early steps that women have taken toward becoming full-fledged people. To do so, women inevitably are changing the most deep-seated patterns of life. Women are in action in ways we've never seen before. They're entering new territory, both literally and psychologically. In doing this, they are raising conflict to a new and more conscious level and searching for better ways to deal with it.

In our individual lives, all relationships must encompass conflict. Whenever two people interact with each other, each person is presenting something new to the other, something different from what would arise from within herself or himself. Our ability to engage with that new thought and feeling is the source of our growth and the growth of the relationship between us. Women have a great desire to engage with others. This desire can be a source of strength in conflict. The best conflicts are those that lead to more and better connection rather than disconnection. This kind of conflict leads to growth, but both (or all) of the people involved have to be ready to enter into this form of conflict. Women have a history of faith in connections. Our best course lies in valuing this history as we face the conflicts that lie before us.

epilogue:
yes, but —

One of the points about the word *insight* as it is generally used in psychology is that we really begin to understand something only *after* we have already begun to change it — a symptom, a character trait, a way of living. Until then, we cannot really *see* it. Because women have begun to change their situation, we can now perceive new ways of understanding women. We begin to see all that was contained within women's second-class status — not only for women but for the entire structuring of the human mind and for our attempts to understand how that structure comes about.

It is apparent that I have tried to be suggestive rather than definitive here. I think of this book as one step in a process in which many people participate. Several people have heard some of these ideas and have helped me with them all along the way. One woman's response strikes me as very pertinent. She said, "I kept wanting to say to you, 'Yes, but . . .' and 'No, you didn't take into account . . .'" If we can keep doing this for each other, we will continue to refine, revise, and eventually recast our ideas altogether. We now have a large community of women and enlightened men who are doing this. This is a new phenomenon.

Today we see that the task of rethinking is more complex than many women may have predicted. Thinking our way through these complexities is not easy. Among the thoughts that women wrote to me after reading this book was that they "felt they had always known these things but hadn't put them into words," "hadn't laid them out where they could

look at them." While I feel grateful personally for these con-
firming words, I believe there is a more important guide
contained in them. There are many things that women
know but have not yet put into words. The powerful reasons
why women have not done so are still with us. Many of us
— although fewer than in the past — are still plagued by the
thought that we can't be on a useful track if we are saying
things that don't coincide with what's been said or what
we've been told about how we should experience something.

It is important that women start from their own experience, especially when it may not "make sense." As women
continue to do so, I think we will find that the prevalent
systems of thought are inadequate. Even the words available
will be inappropriate, both the scientific and the common
words. It makes sense that they would be.

To say this does not mean that all women are always
"right" about everything. It does mean that we can create
a climate for ongoing elucidation. We can critique each
other's thinking and foster a deepening dialogue. This,
I believe, is our hope for the future.

notes

Foreword to the Second Edition

1. See, for example, *Developing a National Agenda to Address Women's Mental Health Needs: A Conference Report,* sponsored by the American Psychological Association, Women and Health Roundtable, and the Federation of Organizations for Professional Women (Washington, D.C.: American Psychological Association, 1985); U.S. Department of Health and Human Services, *Women's Health: Report of the Public Health Service Task Force on Women's Health Issues,* vol. 1 (Washington, D.C.: Public Health Reports, 1985); Jessie Bernard, *The Female World* (New York: Free Press, 1981); and "Women's Mental Health in Times of Transition," in Lenore Walker, ed., *Women and Mental Health Policy* (Beverly Hills, Calif.: Sage, 1984); M. T. S. Mednick, M. Safir, D. Israel, and J. Bernard, eds., *Women's World: The New Scholarship* (New York: Praeger, 1984); Grace K. Baruch, Rosalind C. Barnett, and Caryl Rivers, *Lifeprints: New Patterns of Love and Work for Today's Women* (New York: McGraw-Hill, 1983); Brunetta Wolfman, "Women and Their Many Roles," *Work in Progress,* No. 7 (Wellesley: Stone Center Working Paper Series, 1983).

2. Beth Milwid, "Breaking In: Experiences in Male-Dominated Professions," in Joan H. Robbins and Rachel J. Siegel, eds., *Women Changing Therapy* (New York: Harrington Park Press, 1985).

3. Ibid. See also Irene Stiver, "Work Inhibitions in Women," *Work in Progress,* No. 3 (Wellesley: Stone Center Working Paper Series, 1982); and Judith Jordan, "The Meaning of Mutuality," *Work in Progress,* No. 23 (Wellesley: Stone Center Working Paper Series, 1986).

4. Deborah Belle, *Lives in Stress* (Beverly Hills, Calif.: Sage, 1982); Barbara F. Reskin and Heidi I. Hartmann, eds., *Women's Work, Men's Work* (Washington, D.C.: National Academy Press, 1986).

5. Examples of some of these writings are Toni Cade Bambara, *The*

Black Woman (New York: New American Library, 1970); Susan Cox, *Female Psychology: The Emerging Self* (New York: St. Martin's Press, 1981); Angela Davis, *Women, Class, and Race* (New York: Random House, 1981); Guadalupe Gibson, "Hispanic Women: Stress and Mental Health Issues," in Joan H. Robbins and Rachel J. Siegel, eds., *Women Changing Therapy* (New York: Harrington Park Press, 1985); Pauline Huston, *Third World Women Speak Out* (New York: Praeger, 1978); ISIS Women's International Information and Communication Service, *Women in Development: A Resource Guide for Organization and Action* (Philadelphia: New Society Publishers, 1984); Joyce Ladner, *Tomorrow's Tomorrow* (Garden City, N.Y.: Anchor, 1972); E. Olmedo and D. Parron, "Mental Health of Minority Women," *Professional Psychology* 12 (1981), 103–111; Christine R. Robinson, "Black Women: A Tradition of Self-Reliant Strength," in Joan H. Robbins and Rachel J. Siegel, eds., *Women Changing Therapy* (New York: Harrington Park Press, 1985); L. Rodgers-Rose, *The Black Woman* (Beverly Hills, Calif.: Sage, 1980); Patricia Scott, Barbara Smith, and Gloria Hull, *But Some of Us Are Brave* (Old Westbury, Conn.: Feminist Press, 1981); Clevonne Turner, "Psychosocial Barriers to Black Women's Career Development," *Work in Progress*, No. 15 (Wellesley: Stone Center Working Paper Series, 1984); Phyllis Wallace, *Black Women in the Labor Force* (Cambridge: MIT Press, 1980).

6. See, for example, Barbara Ehrenreich, *The Hearts of Men: American Dreams and the Flight from Commitment* (New York: Doubleday, 1983).

7. Jean Baker Miller, "Women and Power," *Work in Progress*, No. 1 (Wellesley: Stone Center Working Paper Series, 1982).

8. Jean Baker Miller, "The Development of Women's Sense of Self," *Work in Progress*, No. 12 (Wellesley: Stone Center Working Paper Series, 1984).

9. Jean Baker Miller, "What Do We Mean by Relationships?" *Work in Progress*, No. 22 (Wellesley: Stone Center Working Paper Series, 1986).

10. There are many women working on this creative edge in several fields. Examples of only some of these writings in psychology, psychotherapy, and closely related areas are Mary F. Belenky, Blythe M. Clinchy, Nancy R. Goldberger, and Jill M. Tarule, *Women's Way of Knowing* (New York: Basic Books, 1986); Boston Women's Health Book Collective, *Our Bodies, Ourselves*, 2nd ed. (New York: Simon & Schuster, 1985); Paula Caplan, *The Myth of Women's Masochism* (New York: Dutton, 1985); Elizabeth Dodson-Gray, *Patriarchy as a Conceptual Trap* (Wellesley: Roundtable Press, 1982); Barbara Ehrenreich and Deidre English, *For Her Own Good: 150 Years of Experts' Advice to Women* (Garden City, N.Y.: Anchor, 1979); Carol Gilligan, *In a Different Voice: Psychological Theory and Women's Development*

(Cambridge: Harvard University Press, 1982); Judith Jordan, "The Meaning of Mutuality," *Work in Progress,* No. 23 (Wellesley: Stone Center Working Paper Series, 1986) and "Empathy and Self Boundaries," *Work in Progress,* No. 16 (Wellesley: Stone Center Working Paper Series, 1984); Judith Jordan, Janet Surrey, and Alexandra Kaplan, "Women and Empathy," *Work in Progress,* No. 2 (Wellesley: Stone Center Working Paper Series, 1982); Margaret McIntosh, "Feeling Like a Fraud," *Work in Progress,* No. 18 (Wellesley: Stone Center Working Paper Series, 1984); Adrienne Rich, *On Lies, Secrets, and Silence: Selected Prose, 1966–1978* (New York: Norton, 1979), *Of Woman Born* (New York: Bantam, 1976), and "Compulsive Heterosexuality and Lesbian Experience," *Signs* 5(4) (1980), 631–660; Sara Ruddick, "Maternal Thinking," in Barrie Thorne and Marilyn Yalom, eds., *Rethinking the Family* (New York: Longman, 1982); Irene Stiver, "Beyond the Oedipus Complex: Mothers and Daughters," *Work in Progress,* No. 26 (Wellesley: Stone Center Working Paper Series, 1986), "The Meaning of Care: Reframing Treatment Models," *Work in Progress,* No. 20 (Wellesley: Stone Center Working Paper Series, 1985), and "The Meanings of 'Dependency' in Female-Male Relationships," *Work in Progress,* No. 11 (Wellesley: Stone Center Working Paper Series, 1983); Janet Surrey, "The 'Self-in-Relation': A Theory of Women's Development," *Work in Progress,* No. 13 (Wellesley: Stone Center Working Paper Series, 1984).

Many other women have added to our understanding of women's lives. I am noting here only some examples of work that moves beyond prior theoretical assumptions.

11. See, for example, E. Bass and L. Thornton, *I Never Told Anyone: Writings by Women Survivors of Child Sexual Abuse* (New York: Harper & Row, 1983); Pauline Bart, *Stopping Rape* (New York: Pergamon, 1985); Wini Breines and Linda Gordon, "The New Scholarship on Family Violence," *Signs* 8 (1983), 490–531; Susan Brownmiller, *Against Our Will: Men, Women and Rape* (New York: Simon & Schuster, 1975); Ann Burgess and Linda Holmstrom, *Rape: Crisis and Recovery* (Baltimore: R. J. Brady, 1979); Sandra Butler, *Conspiracy of Silence* (San Francisco: Glide, 1978); Judith Herman, *Father-Daughter Incest* (Cambridge: Harvard University Press, 1981); Del Martin, *Battered Wives* (San Francisco: Glide, 1976); T. McNaron and Y. Morgan, *Voices in the Night: Women Speaking About Incest* (Minneapolis: Cleis Press, 1982); Florence Rush, *The Best Kept Secret: Sexual Abuse of Children* (Englewood Cliffs, N.J.: Prentice-Hall, 1980); Carolyn Swift, "Stopping the Violence: Prevention Strategies for Families," in L. A. Bond and B. M. Wagner, eds., *Families in Transition: Primary Prevention Strategies That Work* (Beverly Hills, Calif.: Sage, forthcoming in 1987) and

"Women and Violence: Breaking the Connection," *Work in Progress*, No. 28 (Wellesley: Stone Center Working Paper Series, 1986); Lenore E. Walker, *The Battered Woman* (New York: Harper & Row, 1979) and *The Battered Woman Syndrome* (New York: Springer, 1984).

12. Diane Russell, *Sexual Exploitation: Rape, Child Sexual Abuse and Workplace Harassment* (Beverly Hills, Calif.: Sage, 1984) and *The Secret Trauma* (New York: Basic Books, 1986).

13. *Attorney General's Task Force on Family Violence: Final Report* (Washington, D.C.: U.S. Government Printing Office, 1984); R. E. Dobash and R. Dobash, *Violence Against Wives: A Case Against the Patriarchy* (New York: Free Press, 1979); D. Finkelhor, R. J. Gelles, G. Hotaling, and M. Strauss, *The Dark Side of Families: Current Family Violence Research* (Beverly Hills, Calif.: Sage, 1983); Elaine Hilberman, "The Wife-Beater's Wife Reconsidered," *American Journal of Psychiatry* 137 (1980), 1336–1347.

14. Diane Russell, op. cit.

15. Judith Herman, op. cit., and "Sexual Violence," *Work in Progress*, No. 8 (Wellesley: Stone Center, Working Paper Series, 1983).

PART I

Chapter 1

1. There have been many earlier presentations of similar ideas with somewhat different emphases. See Gunnar Myrdal, "A Parallel to the Negro Problem," Appendix 5 in *An American Dilemma* (New York: Harper, 1944), pp. 1073–78; and Helen Mayer Hacker, "Women as a Minority Group," *Social Forces* 30 (October 1951), 60–69.

PART II

Introduction

1. I have not followed all of Robbins' specific formulations but have presented observations from my own work. Robbins' ideas were presented at a psychoanalytic symposium in 1950, a bleak period for women. It is interesting to note that the colleague who was asked to comment on the paper responded with ridicule and dismissal. The paper was made available only in a small printing of the proceedings of the symposium and never published more widely. Bernard S. Robbins, "The Nature of Fem-

ininity," *Proceedings of Symposium on Feminine Psychology,* sponsored by the Comprehensive Course in Psychoanalysis (New York: New York Medical College, 1950).

Chapter 4

1. John Bowlby, *Attachment and Loss,* Vol. 1, 2, 3 (New York: Basic Books, 1969, 1973, 1980).

2. Jessie Bernard, *Women and the Public Interest: An Essay on Policy and Protest* (Chicago: Aldine-Atherton, 1971).

3. I. Broverman, D. Broverman, et al., "Sex-Role Stereotypes and Clinical Judgments of Mental Health," *Journal of Consulting and Clinical Psychology* 34 (1970), 1–7.

4. Sigmund Freud, "Analysis Terminable and Interminable" (1937), in the *Standard Edition of the Complete Works of Sigmund Freud* (London: Hogarth Press, 1964).

Chapter 5

1. See, for example, Sara Ruddick, "Maternal Thinking," in Barrie Thorne and Marilyn Yalom, eds., *Rethinking the Family* (New York: Longman, 1982) and Adrienne Rich, *Of Woman Born* (New York: W. W. Norton, 1976).

2. Anita Mishler, personal communication.

3. Specific examples of this were pointed out by Clara Thompson and Frieda Fromm-Reichmann long ago. See, for instance, Clara Thompson, "Some Effects of the Derogatory Attitude Towards Female Sexuality," *Psychiatry* 13 (1950), 349–54, reprinted in J. B. Miller, ed., *Psychoanalysis and Women* (New York: Brunner/Mazel, 1973, and Penguin Books, 1973); and Frieda Fromm-Reichmann and Virginia Gunst, "Discussion of Dr. Thompson's Paper," reprinted in *ibid.*

4. Paula Caplan, *The Myth of Women's Masochism* (New York: E.P. Dutton, 1985).

Chapter 6

1. See, for example, Harriet Lerner, "Early Origins of Envy and Devaluation of Women: Implications for Sex Role Stereotypes," *Bulletin of the Menninger Clinic,* 38 (1974), 538–53, and Jean Baker Miller, "Intimacy

in Relation to Work and Family," *Journal of Psychiatric Treatment and Evaluation* 3 (1981), 123–129, and Irene Stiver, "The Meanings of 'Dependency' in Female-Male Relationships," *Work in Progress*, No. 11 (Wellesley: Stone Center Working Paper Series, 1983).

2. J. Money and A. Ehrhardt, *Man and Woman, Boy and Girl* (Baltimore: Johns Hopkins University Press, 1973), and J. Brooks-Gunn and W. S. Mathews, *He and She: How Children Develop Their Sex-Role Identity* (Englewood Cliffs, N.J.: Spectrum, 1979), and E. Tobach and B. Rossoff, *Genes and Gender*, vols. 1, 2, and 3 (New York: Gordian Press, 1978, 1979, 1980).

Chapter 7

1. See, for instance, Michelle Z. Rosaldo, "Women, Culture, and Society: A Theoretical Overview"; Nancy Chodorow, "Family Structure and Feminine Personality"; and Sherry B. Ortner, "Is Female to Male as Nature Is to Culture?"—all in M.Z. Rosaldo and L. Lamphere, *Women, Culture, and Society* (Stanford: Stanford University Press, 1974).

2. David Bakan, *The Duality of Human Existence* (Boston: Beacon Press, 1966).

3. Christopher Lasch, " 'Selfish Women': The Campaign to Save the American Family, 1890–1920," *The Columbia University Forum* (Spring 1975), 23–31.

PART III

Chapter 8

1. In the first edition of this book I used the word *affiliation* throughout this chapter and others. Since then, many people have used the word *connection*. Carol Gilligan, especially, has made the word central in her formulations. I think it is a much better word and have substituted it for affiliation in many places here. C. Gilligan, *In a Different Voice: Psychological Theory and Women's Development* (Cambridge, Mass.: Harvard University Press, 1982).

2. Jean Baker Miller, "The Development of Women's Sense of Self," *Work in Progress*, No. 12 (Wellesley: Stone Center Working Paper Series, 1984).

3. Walter Bonime, "The Psychodynamics of Neurotic Depression," in Silvano Arieti, ed., *American Handbook of Psychiatry*, vol. 3 (New York: Basic Books, 1966).

4. Jean Baker Miller and Stephen M. Sonnenberg, "Depression Following Psychotic Episodes: A Response to the Challenge of Change?" *Journal of the American Academy of Psychoanalysis* 1 (1973), 253–70.

5. Alexandra Kaplan, " 'The Self in Relation': Implications for Depression in Women," *Work in Progress*, No. 14 (Wellesley: Stone Center Working Paper Series, 1984).

Chapter 9

1. Teresa Bernardez, "Women and Anger: Conflicts with Aggression in Contemporary Women," *Journal of the American Medical Women's Association* 33 (1978), 215–219; Jean Baker Miller, "The Construction of Anger in Women and Men," *Work in Progress*, No. 4 (Wellesley: Stone Center Working Paper Series, 1983); Harriet Lerner, *The Dance of Anger: A Woman's Guide to Changing the Pattern of Intimate Relationships* (New York: Harper & Row, 1985).

2. M. Wertheimer, *Productive Thinking* (New York: Harper, 1959).

Chapter 10

1. Jean Baker Miller, "Women and Power," *Work in Progress*, No. 1 (Wellesley: Stone Center Working Paper Series, 1982).

2. David C. McClelland, *Power: The Inner Experience* (New York: Irvington, 1979).

3. Elizabeth Janeway, *The Powers of the Weak* (New York: Knopf, 1980).

Chapter 11

1. The Women's Self-Help Network, *Working Together for Change: Women's Self-Help Handbook*, vols. 1 and 2 (Campbell River, British Columbia: Ptarmigian Press, 1984).

2. Deborah Belle, *Lives in Stress* (Beverly Hills, Calif.: Sage, 1982); Barbara F. Reskin and Heidi I. Hartmann, eds., *Women's Work, Men's Work* (Washington, D.C.: National Academy Press, 1986).

3. Adrienne Rich, "Compulsive Heterosexuality and Lesbian Experience," *Signs* 5(4) (1980), 631–660.

4. Some examples of this extensive work are Nanette Gartrell, "Issues in Psychotherapy with Lesbian Women," *Work in Progress*, No. 10 (Wellesley: Stone Center Working Paper Series, 1983) and "Gay Patients in the Medical Setting," in C. Nadelson and D. Marcotte, eds., *Treatment Interventions in Human Sexuality* (New York: Plenum, 1983); A. Martin, "Some

Issues in the Treatment of Gay and Lesbian Patients," *Psychotherapy: Theory, Research and Practice* 19(3) (1982), 341–348; Del Martin and Phyllis Lyon, "Lesbian Women and Mental Health Policy," in Lenore Walker, ed., *Women and Mental Health Policy* (Beverly Hills, Calif.: Sage, 1984); Adrienne Rich, op. cit.; G. Vida, ed., *Our Right to Love* (Englewood Cliffs, N.J.: Prentice-Hall, 1978).

5. See, for example, Beverly Birns, "The Mother-Infant Tie: 50 Years of Theory, Science and Science Fiction," *Work in Progress*, No. 21 (Wellesley: Stone Center Working Paper Series, 1985); Stella Chess, "Blame the Mother Ideology," *International Journal of Mental Health* 11 (1972), 95–107; Stella Chess and Alexander Thomas, "Infant Bonding: Mystique and Reality," *American Journal of Orthopsychiatry* 52 (1982), 213–222; Helen Block Lewis and Judith Lewis Herman, "Anger in the Mother-Daughter Relationship," in T. Bernay and D. W. Cantro, eds., *The Psychology of Today's Woman: New Psychoanalytic Visions* (Hillside, N.J.: Lawrence Erlbaum, 1986); Adrienne Rich, *Of Woman Born* (New York: Bantam, 1976); Sara Ruddick, "Maternal Thinking," in Barrie Thorne and Marilyn Yalom, eds., *Rethinking the Family* (New York: Longman, 1982); Irene Stiver, "Beyond the Oedipus Complex: Mothers and Daughters," *Work in Progress*, No. 26 (Wellesley: Stone Center Working Paper Series, 1986); Alexander Thomas and Stella Chess, *Temperament and Development* (New York: Brunner/Mazel, 1977).

index

151

JEAN BAKER MILLER earned her B.A. at Sarah Lawrence College and her M.D. at Columbia University. She has been practicing psychiatry and psychoanalysis for thirty years and teaching them for twenty-five, and is currently clinical professor of psychiatry at the School of Medicine, Boston University. Professor Miller was the first director of the Stone Center for Developmental Studies and Services at Wellesley College and is now scholar-in-residence there. She has taught at the London School of Economics, spent two years at the Tavistock Institute and Clinic in London, and served as secretary and trustee of the American Academy of Psychoanalysis, trustee of the American Orthopsychiatric Association, and board member of Women's Action for Nuclear Disarmament and the Elizabeth Stone House, an alternative residential center for women in crisis. Professor Miller has been a member of the Committee on Women's Employment and Related Social Issues of the National Research Council and a recipient of a Rockefeller Foundation Humanities Fellowship. Articles by Professor Miller have appeared in numerous professional journals and her first book, *Psychoanalysis and Women,* was published in 1973. The first edition of *Toward a New Psychology of Women* has been published in nine countries.